A Claremont Management Group Book

ISBN: 979-8-9851962-1-4

ISBN (e-book): 979-8-9851962-0-7

Bad Deal for America

Claremont Management Group, Inc.

Houston, TX

www.ClaremontManagementGroup.com

Published in the United States of America

This book is dedicated to every single taxpayer in America: past, present, and future. It is critical that Americans make their wasteful government work for them and not the other way around.

Table of Contents

Introduction 1

Dealt a Pile of Chips by the Taxpayers 3

Diamonds 15

Steve King 16

Mitch McConnell 20

Jeff Flake 24

Joe Barton 26

Larry Craig 28

Matt Gaetz 30

John Kasich 34

Lindsey Graham 36

Mark Walker 40

Tom DeLay 42

Marjorie Taylor Greene 44

Joe Scarborough 48

Bob Dornan 52

Spades 55

John Kerry 56

Alexandria Ocasio-Cortez.. 60

Amy Klobuchar 64

Harry Reid.. 68

Elizabeth Warren.. 72

Hillary Clinton.. 76

Max Baucus 80

Rashida Tlaib 84

Chris Murphy 88

Jerry Nadler 92

Dianne Feinstein.. 94

Chuck Schumer 96

Adam Schiff 98

Hearts 101

Mo Brooks 102

Don Young 106

Newt Gingrich 110

Glenn Grothman 114

Ted Cruz...118

Jesse Helms 122

Orrin Hatch...126

Todd Akin...130

Rick Santorum 134

Mitt Romney 138

Michele Bachmann..142

Chuck Grassley 146

Dan Quayle...150

Clubs **153**

Alcee Hastings..154

Ilhan Omar..158

Maxine Waters..162

Ayanna Pressley 166

Karen Bass..170

Eddie Bernice Johnson 172

John Edwards 174

Cori Bush..176

Sheila Jackson Lee..180

Al Franken...184

Nancy Pelosi 188

Bernie Sanders 192

Kamala Harris...196

Joe Biden...201

Other "Chips" 210

Red Chips..210

Blue Chips 213

Cashing in their Chips......................................216

Conclusion 230

Public Records Access on Member Financial Reports 231

Acknowledgements...232

About the Author...233

Introduction

This is a book to make each and every American think about the people they have elected to the House and Senate of the United States. While there are losers in every level of government, this book is limited to those presently serving or who have served in either or both houses of Congress. To make the book more relevant, the focus has been on those who have recently served, although there are a few who have been on the public dole for 30, 40 and 50 years.

In popular parlance today, Democrats are Blue, and Republicans are Red. I am really not sure why these colors were selected. However, they are so frequently used today that it seemed appropriate to have the Diamonds and Hearts in red, reserved for Republicans, and Clubs and Spades in Blue, reserved for Democrats.

The initial chapter details, as best as can be determined, the pay and benefits for members of Congress. This is followed by short chapters, "The Cards," featuring the con-artists, liars, fraudsters, philanderers, and other miscreants who have somehow won election to these high offices. Yes, there are many who are in Congress or who have previously served, who are some of the best people on earth. Yet, the election to Congress seems to blight even the best of them. Some featured in this book simply had the misfortune to have stupid statements caught by a reporter or a TV camera. They can use this sentence to explain to their constituents why they ended up in this book. Being included in this book is certainly not intended to be a badge of honor.

Every effort was made to exactly quote the various news sources used in this book. Each quote has a citation. In short, if anyone featured in this book does not like a particular quote attributed to them, they can take it up with the listed source. Each quote was checked multiple times before this book went to press.

In the research for this book, it is noted that some of the best chose to serve a limited number of terms and went home. All of them should be doing that, of course. Our early elected officers respected the fact that they were "representing" Americans and stayed in touch with their constituents and their home locations. They served a reasonable number of terms and returned home to live under the laws and circumstances they created. Today, most have become polluted by the allure of the attention and spotlight in DC, sort of the Las Vegas for those who win election to Congress. Many who leave Congressional office stay in the overpriced suburbs of DC and the townhouses of Georgetown to rake in even more money as lobbyists and influence peddlers.

There is a point to this book. Americans desperately need term limits for members of Congress, and they need to elect people of honor, intelligence and integrity. The majority of those serving in Congress have been there too long and lost touch with their constituents. If this book does not drive the members to shorten their time in DC, perhaps the American people will get organized and finally implement term limits across the board for all elected officials at all levels. Some states and localities have implemented terms limits, but this has not become universal and has not become law at the federal level.

David D. Schein

Houston, Texas

Dealt a Pile of Chips by the Taxpayers

While members of both houses of Congress will proclaim that they are underpaid and overworked, most Americans would probably disagree if they saw their combined pay and benefits. There is a reason that these elected representatives cling to these positions for decades, and it is not just due to the quest for power and access to TV cameras. The facts are listed below along with the latest publicly available data.

Salary

The current base congressional salary for most Senators, Representatives, Delegates, and the Resident Commissioner from Puerto Rico is $174,000 per year.[1] The Speaker of the House gets $223,500 per year.[2] To put this in perspective, the average net US compensation is a fraction of the Congressional

---

[1] https://crsreports.congress.gov/product/pdf/RL/97-615 (page 2)
[2] https://www.senate.gov/CRSpubs/9c14ec69-c4e4-4bd8-8953-f73daa1640e4.pdf

base salary at $51,916.27 and a more realistic figure is the median of $34,248.45 (as of 2019).[3]

Representatives and Senators will claim that they are dramatically underpaid due to needing a home in very expensive Washington, D.C. and in their home district. Notwithstanding the fact that the median net worth of these "public servants" is $1,092,767 (2018), with Senators at $1,696,020 (2018) and Representatives at $489,514 (2018). This ranges from $214,092,575, John Warner (D-VA) to an incredible -$7,549,002 Alcee Hastings (D-FL).[4] Perhaps reducing their salaries to the national average is really what the doctor ordered? They serve for decades with little connection or accountability to their home constituents. "The average length of service for Representatives at the beginning of the 117th Congress was 8.9 years (4.5 House terms); for Senators, 11.0 years (1.8 Senate terms)."[5] The statistics of the increase in the length of time in office are clear:

> The prior House service of incoming Representatives increased from an average of 2.5 years in the 19th century to 9.4 in the 21st to date; the average peaked at 10.3 years—just over five terms—during the 102nd (1991-1992), 110th (2007-2008), and 111th Congresses (2009-2010). Incoming Senators averaged 4.8 years of prior chamber service in the 19th century, and 11.2 years during the 21st century to date. This figure peaked at 13.1 years during the 111th Congress (2009-2010).[6]

Unfortunately, absent a serious effort by the citizens to pass term limit legislation, this trend will likely continue.

The United States has just come through the worst public health crisis in 100 years and many employees proved that they

---

[3] https://www.ssa.gov/oact/cola/central.html
[4] https://www.opensecrets.org/personal-finances
[5] https://crsreports.congress.gov/product/pdf/R/R46705 (page 2)
[6] https://fas.org/sgp/crs/misc/R41545.pdf

could work successfully from home. It is time for these elected officials to remain based in their home districts and not where highly paid lobbyists and special interest groups can assert excessive influence over them. In fact, some of the most obnoxious members of Congress have illustrated that they do not need to buy a residence in D.C.[7]

Outside Earned Income Limits

Permissible "outside earned income" for Representatives and Senators is limited to 15% of the annual rate of basic pay for Level II of the Executive Schedule.[8] This calculates to $28,440 per year for 2019, or by itself close to the median net income for Americans. Given the growth of the net worth of many of these representatives while in D.C., other sources are obviously in play. See the "Cashing in their Chips" chapter later in this book.

An Extra Tip

Each member is entitled to a $3,000 per year tax reduction for living expenses.[9]

First Class Travel

Of course, members get to travel in style on Americans' tax dollars[10]. For most corporate employees, there must be a business reason for each trip charged to corporate expense accounts. There is little accountability for these Congressional trips, covered under the affectionate title of "Boondoggles." If total transparency was required for all member expenses, perhaps by a "citizens' review panel" made up of constituents for each member, many of these trips might be eliminated.

---

[7] See: https://www.cnn.com/2013/12/04/politics/real-alpha-house

[8] https://www.federalregister.gov/documents/2021/01/06/2021-00040/adjustments-of-certain-rates-of-pay

[9] https://crsreports.congress.gov/product/pdf/RL/RL30064 (page 3).

[10]

https://www.usatoday.com/story/news/politics/2017/02/27/taxpayers-fund-first-class-congressional-foreign-travel-boom-overseas/98351442/

Members' Representational Allowance ("MRA")

This is a budget authorized by the Committee on House Administration for each House Member in support of the conduct of their official and representational duties for their district.[11] When outside observers comment on the high cost of Congress, often mentioned is the MRA. This generous and largely unregulated slush fund is for supporting personnel, office expenses, travel to their districts, and of course, free mail so they can proclaim to their constituents all the great things they are doing for them.[12] In 2019, MRAs ranged from $1,320,585 to $1,498,546, per Member, with an average of $1,382,329. This amount has been steadily increasing since 2014.

The MRA is funded in the House "Salaries and Expenses" account in the annual legislative branch appropriations bills. For 2020, this amounted to $615.0 million, a 7.2% increase from 2019. This does not include $11.025 million budget allowance in 2020 for interns.[13] Naturally, if the D.C. offices were cut to the bone in one of America's costliest cities, these Members could stay closer to their constituents and cut their overhead dramatically.

Senators' Official Personnel and Office Expense Account ("SOPOEA")

Supporting personnel, office expenses, and mail for Senators involves a substantial amount for each fiscal year. The preliminary list of SOPOEA levels contained in the Senate report accompanying the FY2020 legislative branch appropriations bill[14] shows a range of $3,436,535 to $5,421,200, with the average allowance of $3,738,775. For 2020, this amounts to

---

[11] https://www.house.gov/the-house-explained/open-government/statement-of-disbursements/frequently-asked-questions
[12] https://crsreports.congress.gov/product/pdf/RL/RL30064 (page 4)
[13] The distribution of this money is explained at https://www.house.gov/the-house-explained/open-government/statement-of-disbursements
[14] (S. 2581, S.Rept. 116-124)

$449 million, almost half a billion dollars, and marks a 4.7% increase from 2019, but at least it includes the allowance for interns.[15]

Up to $40,000 to Furnish Office Space

Despite the fact that the Capitol offices belong to the "people" and office furniture does not change that much over time, apparently each member can spend up to $40,000 on new furniture per year.[16] Most working Americans are issued furniture already owned by their employer and there does not seem to be any pressing need for the taxpayers to repurchase basic office furniture repeatedly for Members.[17]

Congressional Retirement Benefits

Often mentioned as one of the most compelling reasons to rein-in Congressional spending is the generous retirement benefits. Members serving before 1984 did not have to participate in Social Security. Prior to 1984, they were instead covered by the Civil Service Retirement System ("CSRS"), which granted them much greater pensions. Members elected after 1984 are covered by both Social Security and the Federal Employees' Retirement System, ("FERS"). "All Senators and those Representatives serving as Members prior to September 30, 2003, may decline [FERS]. Representatives entering office on or after September 30, 2003, cannot elect to be excluded from such coverage. Members who were already in Congress when Social Security coverage went into effect could either remain in CSRS or change their coverage to FERS."[18]

There are different retirement plans for Members as noted below:

---

[15] https://crsreports.congress.gov/product/pdf/RL/RL30064 (page 7)

[16] https://www.house.gov/the-house-explained/open-government/statement-of-disbursements/frequently-asked-questions

[17] https://www.senate.gov/CRSpubs/ac0d1dd5-7316-4390-87e6-353589586a89.pdf

[18] https://www.senate.gov/CRSpubs/ac0d1dd5-7316-4390-87e6-353589586a89.pdf (page 2)

- Coverage: This is full coverage by both CSRS and Social Security.
- CSRS Offset: This is coverage by CSRS and Social Security, but with CSRS contributions and benefits reduced (offset) by the amount of Social Security contributions and benefits.
- FERS is composed of three elements:
- Social Security;
- The FERS basic annuity, a monthly pension based on years of service and the average of the three highest consecutive years of basic pay; and
- The Thrift Savings Plan, into which participants can deposit up to a maximum of $19,000 in 2019. Note that participants who are at least age 50 in 2019 can make an additional catch-up contribution of up to $6,000. Their employing agency matches employee contributions up to 5% of pay[19].
- Social Security Only: This occurs if the Member declines other coverage. Obviously, it is unclear why any Member or their staffers would take this option.

Of particular note is the FERS. Members and staffers are eligible for a pension at the age of 62 if they have completed at least five years of service. They are eligible for a pension at age 50 if they have completed 20 years of service. And, they are eligible at any age after completing 25 years of service. The starting amount of a Member's retirement annuity may not exceed 80% of his or her final salary.

To put this in perspective, 617 retired Members of Congress are receiving federal pensions based fully or in part on their congressional service as of October 1, 2018. Of these, 318 had retired under CSRS and were receiving an average annual pension of $75,528 (2018). An additional 299 Members had retired with service under FERS and were receiving an

---

[19] https://crsreports.congress.gov/product/pdf/RL/RL30387

average annual pension of $41,208 (2018).[20] Again, these benefits are in addition to Social Security based on their substantial Congressional salaries and their Thrift Plan savings.

This confusing mix helps hide the fact that Members and most Federal employees, including the Congressional staffers, enjoy this generous mix of retirement benefits, which far exceed the benefits for the average American taxpayer. Median private pensions and annuities in 2019 was only $10,788, and only one-third of older Americans even receive pensions.[21] This is paired with an estimated annual average Social Security benefit for 2021 of $18,516.[22]

Congressional Gym

Naturally, the benefits do not stop with the above listing. Of interest is that there is a Congressional gym and House members pay $20/month and Senators pay $40/month.[23] These amounts are significantly less than the cost of a private gym membership in the D.C. area. Of course, most Members do not look like they have been inside a gym in years.

Using Campaign Funds for Personal Use

It is illegal to use campaign funds for personal use. However, this area is hard to regulate, so it is widely regarded by outside observers as another slush fund for potential Member abuse. The "Irrespective Test" is the main benchmark to distinguish a campaign expense from a personal expense.[24] The basic idea is that if the politician would have spent the money anyway, "irrespective of campaigning," it is a personal expense. If it is clearly related to a campaign, then campaign

---

[20] https://www.senate.gov/CRSpubs/ac0d1dd5-7316-4390-87e6-353589586a89.pdf (page 2)

[21] http://www.pensionrights.org/publications/statistic/income-pensions

[22] https://www.aarp.org/retirement/social-security/questions-answers/how-much-social-security-will-i-get.html

[23] https://abcnews.go.com/Politics/members-house-gym-subsidized-taxpayers/story?id=13839542

[24] https://www.fec.gov/help-candidates-and-committees/making-disbursements/personal-use/

9

funds can be used for those expenses. But read on for more explanation of how this can creatively be used by present and former Members, as well as candidates for Congress. Some of the details may surprise the reader.

For instance, here are some expenses that are not considered "personal" expenses:

- **Charitable donations:** The one caveat is that the donations cannot be somehow used to personally benefit the candidate.
- **Transfer of campaign assets:** "The sale or transfer of a campaign asset to either the candidate or a third party does not constitute personal use as long as the transaction is made at the fair market value."[25]
- **Gifts:** Candidates can make gifts of "nominal value" to non-family members.
- **Candidate Salary:** This is the most surprising non-personal use. A candidate can receive a salary from his or her campaign. The rules are fairly simple in that it must be paid from the "principal campaign committee," and is limited to the lower of the annual salary for the position being sought or what the candidate made the prior year. Incumbents are not eligible for this payment and salary for less than a full year must be pro-rated. The end of this gravy train is the date of the general election, or if a run-off, when that election takes place. A sidenote on this is that family members can be employed in a campaign and paid from the campaign coffers.

On the flip side are things that will be considered personal use without further analysis. This includes:

- **Household food items and supplies:** So, normal household groceries and supplies are considered personal. But the campaign may pay for food and

---

[25] https://www.fec.gov/help-candidates-and-committees/making-disbursements/personal-use/

10

supplies for fundraising activities and campaign meetings, even if held in the candidate's home. Leftovers anyone?

- **Funeral and burial expenses:** This seems obvious that the candidate cannot use campaign funds for such family expenses. However, they may use such funds to "cover funeral, cremation and burial expenses for a candidate or campaign worker whose death arises out of, or in the course of, campaign activity." This could be considered the Chicago provision.
- **Clothing:** Normal day-to-day clothes are excluded, but the campaign can pay for campaign-related swag.
- **Tuition Payments:** Normally, campaign funds cannot be used to pay for tuition, however, if related to training the campaign workers, then that is a permitted use. A candidate even received permission to take Spanish lessons to communicate with some of her constituents.[26]
- **Mortgage, Rent and Utility Payments:** Rather obviously, such expenses for the candidate's personal residence are not included. Interestingly, if there are security concerns for the candidate, they can use campaign funds to upgrade the security system in their residence.
- **Investment expenses:** Investments to enhance the campaign funds available are permitted, as long as they are not for personal use. This type of provision would appear to have an open door for abuse.
- **Entertainment:** Normal admission for entertainment and sporting events are considered personal. However, a campaign can hold an event at such a venue, which would convert it to a campaign expense.

---

[26] https://www.fec.gov/files/legal/aos/1997-11/1997-11.pdf

- **Dues, Fees and Gratuities:** Campaign funds cannot be used for such personal expenses, but it does not take a lot of imagination to see how many such expenses could be attributed to campaigns.
- **Case-by-case Determination of Personal Use:** For cases not listed above, the Federal Election Commission, "FEC," will make a determination on a case-by-case basis. That is, of course, if it ever comes before the Commission. These include travel expenses, vehicle expenses, and legal expenses.
- **Promotion of Candidate's Books:** Given some of the large advances and other payments to various Members for writing books, this would hardly seem to be an issue. And indeed, these expenses are not supposed to be paid from the campaign treasury. However, promotion of the candidates' books can be a campaign expense.[27]

Some of the recently elected Members have run afoul of the campaign rules above. Recent reports of violations include Ilhan Omar,[28] Rashida Tlaib,[29] and of course the highest profile member of "The Squad," Alexandria Ocasio-Cortez.[30] In an odd twist on the use of campaign funds:

> *New York Democratic Rep. Alexandria Ocasio-Cortez invested a large sum of money into political merchandise for her online store since the start of 2021, Reuters reported Monday. The merchandise includes items with slogans such as "AOC," "Tax the Rich," and "Fight for our Future." Ocasio-Cortez'*

---

[27] https://www.fec.gov/help-candidates-and-committees/making-disbursements/personal-use/
[28] https://www.foxnews.com/politics/omar-hit-with-fec-complaint-for-allegedly-paying-lovers-travel-expenses-with-campaign-funds
[29] https://www.nationalreview.com/news/ethics-probe-into-rashida-tlaib-extended-after-ethics-watchdog-finds-substantial-evidence-of-misuse-of-campaign-funds/
[30] https://www.foxnews.com/politics/ocasio-cortezs-millionaire-chief-of-staff-violated-fec-rules-to-hide-885g-fec-complaint-alleges

campaign paid Financial Innovations, a political merchandise firm, over $1.4 million, according to the Federal Election Commission, Reuters reported. (07/19/21).[31]

AOC, or her handlers, seem to have quickly figured out the campaign finance game. She raised over $21 million for her 2020 campaign and only spent $17 million, leaving her with $4 million. Similarly, in 2018, she raised $2.2 million and only spent $1.8 million.[32]

Abuses, actual and potential, of campaign funds are not limited to current office holders. One report estimated that "42 members of Congress who plan to retire or have already resigned ahead of November's midterm election, and their campaign committee war chests boast a combined $50 million." (02/27/18)[33]. A fascinating January 2018 article in the *Tampa Bay Times* referred to "Zombie Campaigns." In just one campaign fund abuse example, it described campaign consulting fees being paid from the account of a deceased member of Congress over a 17-month period after his death.[34]

An interesting benefit of a campaign fund is to fund a campaign for a completely different office. Mitt Romney demonstrated this in 2018 in his successful run for a US Senate seat from Utah. He transferred $1 million left over in his campaign fund from his unsuccessful 2012 presidential race to

---

[31] https://dailycaller.com/2021/07/19/alexandria-ocasio-cortez-online-store-political-merchandise/

[32] See: https://disclosures-clerk.house.gov/public_disc/financial-pdfs/2018/10026781.pdf ; https://disclosures-clerk.house.gov/public_disc/financial-pdfs/2019/10037907.pdf ; https://www.fec.gov/data/candidate/H8NY15148/?cycle=2018 ; and https://www.fec.gov/data/candidate/H8NY15148/?cycle=2020 .

[33] https://www.opensecrets.org/news/2018/02/cash-on-hand/

[34] https://projects.tampabay.com/projects/2018/investigations/zombie-campaigns/spending-millions-after-office/

his senate campaign fund.[35] This gave him a big advantage over other candidates from either party.

---

[35] https://www.sltrib.com/news/politics/2018/04/10/mitt-romney-transfers-1-million-left-over-from-his-presidential-run-to-his-senate-race-in-utah/

Diamonds

Steve King

Congressman from IA 4th District since 2003

18 years in DC

"What if we went back through all the family trees and just pulled out anyone who was a product of rape or incest? Would there be any population of the world left if we did that? Considering all the wars and all the rapes and pillages that happened throughout all these different nations, I know that I can't say that I was not a part of a product of that." (08/14/19) https://www.theguardian.com/us-news/2019/aug/14/steve-king-iowa-republican-rape-incest-abortion

"We provide drugs through Medicare and Medicaid that are lifesaving drugs; we don't pay for lifestyle drugs... [It is wrong to tell taxpayers that] 'we're going to take the money you earned on overtime to pay for Grandpa's Viagra.'" (06/25/05) https://www.nytimes.com/2005/06/25/politics/house-rejects-coverage-of-impotence-pills.html

"[Global warming is] more of a religion than a science." (08/07/13) https://www.salon.com/2013/08/07/steve_king_global_warming_more_of_a_religion_than_a_science/

"White nationalist, white supremacist, Western civilization — how did that language become offensive?" (01/10/19) https://thehill.com/homenews/house/424688-steve-king-asks-how-terms-white-nationalist-and-white-supremacist-became

"You could look over there and think the Democratic Party is no country for white men." (01/10/19) https://www.nytimes.com/2019/01/11/us/politics/steve-king-republicans-white-supremacy-.html

"The rationale is that if infidels are eating this pork, they aren't eating it, so as long as they're preparing this pork for infidels, it helps send 'em to hell and it'll make Allah happy. I don't want people doing my pork that won't eat it. Let alone hope I'll go to hell for eating pork chops." [doesn't want Muslims packaging his pork] (06/22/18) https://www.cnn.com/2018/06/22/politics/steve-king-muslims-pork/index.html

17

"I'd like to see an America that is just so homogeneous that we look a lot the same." (03/13/17)

https://www.nbcnews.com/politics/politics-news/steve-king-defends-somebody-else-s-babies-remarks-n732741

"I had a strong, Christian lawyer tell me yesterday that, under this decision that he has read, what it brings about is: It only requires one human being in this relationship—that you could marry your lawnmower with this decision. I think he's right." - interprets gay marriage decision as marriage only requires one person now. (07/07/15)

https://slate.com/news-and-politics/2015/07/steve-king-marrying-a-lawnmower-iowa-congressman-imagines-strange-desires.html

Mitch McConnell

Senator from KY since 1985

31 Years in DC

"If I'm still the majority leader of the Senate, think of me as the 'Grim Reaper.'" (04/24/19)
https://www.salon.com/2019/04/24/mcconnell-vows-to-block-democratic-proposals-after-2020-elections-think-of-me-as-the-grim-reaper/

"Breaking the rules to change the rules is un-American." (04/04/19)
https://www.nytimes.com/2019/04/04/opinion/senate-filibuster-mcconnell.html

"One of my proudest moments was when I looked at Barack Obama in the eye and I said, 'Mr. President, you will not fill this Supreme Court vacancy.'" (08/06/16)
https://www.washingtonpost.com/news/powerpost/wp/2016/08/16/the-forgotten-nominee-merrick-garlands-fate-rests-on-forces-beyond-his-control/

"Nobody is happy about losing lives but, remember, these are not draftees. These are full-time professional soldiers." (12/07/07) https://archive.thinkprogress.org/mitch-mcconnell-on-u-s-troop-deaths-1e48b58a4409/

"One hundred percent of my focus is on stopping this new administration." (05/05/21)
https://www.msnbc.com/opinion/mcconnell-dodged-liz-cheney-drama-helped-biden-n1266583

"So my warning, if you will, to corporate America is to stay out of politics." [But] "I'm not talking about political contributions." (04/06/21)
https://www.nbcnews.com/politics/congress/mcconnell-warns-corporate-america-stay-out-politics-says-donations-are-n1263173[36]

---

[36] See also: https://www.opensecrets.org/members-of-congress/mitch-mcconnell/summary?cid=N00003389&cycle=2020&type=P

"Nobody serving in this chamber can even begin — can even begin to imagine — what a completely scorched earth Senate would look like [without the filibuster]."

(03/16/21) https://apnews.com/article/joe-biden-politics-mitch-mcconnell-legislation-filibusters-cdceb62f3a4c8ba933deb246c43de50d

"Borrowing from our grandkids to do socialism for rich people is a terrible way to get help to families who actually need it." (12/31/20) https://www.politico.com/news/2020/12/31/lindsey-graham-mcconnell-separate-vote-2-000-checks-453015

Jeff Flake

Congressman from AZ 1st & 6th Districts from 2001 - 2013

Senator from AZ from 2013 - 2019

18 years in DC

"It was a mistake to limit my own terms." (04/12/06)
https://usatoday30.usatoday.com/news/washington/2006-04-12-term-limits_x.htm

"I did expect to have a primary opponent. I deserve one," he said Tuesday. "By all rights, I ought to have an opponent. I just got lucky, I guess." (07/12/06)
https://www.eastvalleytribune.com/news/flake-faces-solo-race-after-judge-removes-hopeful/article_517cfb47-cd85-53a3-8429-7e6de94c94e8.html

"I think we can all agree that, had we not done so, that the biological and chemical weapons that Saddam Hussein possesses would be added to nuclear weapons which he would certainly possess today had he not been thwarted at that time." (10/08/02) https://www.govinfo.gov/content/pkg/CREC-2002-10-08/html/CREC-2002-10-08-pt1-PgH7268.htm

"Trust me when I say that you can go elsewhere for a job. But you cannot go elsewhere for a soul." [Implied supporting Trump is selling a person's soul] (09/30/19)
https://www.marketwatch.com/story/jeff-flake-urges-fellow-republicans-to-save-your-souls-by-opposing-trump-in-2020-2019-09-30

"I'm saying he [President Trump] borrowed that phrase. It was popularized by Josef Stalin, used by Mao as well — enemy of the people." (01/14/18)
https://www.politico.com/story/2018/01/14/flake-trump-stalin-media-fake-news-340605

Joe Barton

Congressman from TX 6th District from 1985 - 2019
34 years in DC

"You, sir, shut up!" (03/15/17)
https://www.washingtonpost.com/news/powerpost/wp/2017/03/15/you-sir-shut-up-republican-congressman-shouts-down-a-constituent-at-tense-town-hall/?wpisrc=nl_evening&wpmm=1

"I am sorry I did not use better judgment during those days. I am sorry that I let my constituents down." [Apologizing for leaked nude photo.] (11/22/17)
https://www.politico.com/story/2017/11/22/gop-congressman-barton-apologizes-for-nude-selfie-259442

"I want you soo bad. Right now. Deep and hard." [Text message leaked along with nude image of himself.] (11/22/17)
https://www.newsweek.com/republican-congressman-joe-barton-victim-revenge-porn-720235

"men are men...and u r definitely a sexy woman."

"wanna tell me what u r wearing or not wearing tonight miss sweet dreams."

"I dont know about good..but I am married."

[Facebook messages reported.] (10/02/13)
https://www.miamiherald.com/news/nation-world/national/article187115778.html

"You can't regulate God. Not even the Democratic majority in the US Congress can regulate God." (05/19/09)
https://archive.thinkprogress.org/barton-we-shouldnt-regulate-co2-because-it-s-in-your-coca-cola-and-you-can-t-regulate-god-e2720a6709b4/

"If you are familiar with Texas Hold 'Em poker, he doesn't have the nuts. It is not a done deal. Nor do I. ... We will see which has the other by the nuts next week." (05/22/09)
https://archive.thinkprogress.org/after-promising-to-have-waxman-by-the-nuts-joe-barton-whines-about-getting-beat-time-after-time-68e892015e6/

Larry Craig

Congressman from ID 1st District from 1981 - 1991

Senator from ID from 1991 - 2009

28 Years in DC

"Matt, you won't believe this. But I don't use the Internet. I don't have a computer at my desk. I've never used the Internet. It's just not what I do. I e-mail with my BlackBerry. No, I did not know that. I had no reason to know that." (10/16/07)
https://www.youtube.com/watch?v=fwx8sV1LV1A&ab_channel=Veracifier

"The American people already know that Bill Clinton is a bad boy, a naughty boy. I'm going to speak out for the citizens of my state who in the majority think that Bill Clinton is probably even a nasty, bad, naughty boy." (01/24/99)
https://www.motherjones.com/politics/2007/08/senator-larry-craig-r-idaho-busted-public-sex-continuing-gop-trend/

"I'm not gay, and I don't cruise, and I don't hit on men." [I don't] "go around anywhere hitting on men, and by God, if I did, I wouldn't do it in Boise, Idaho! Jiminy!" (09/07/07)
https://abcnews.go.com/Politics/story?id=3573171&page=1

"In June, I overreacted and made a poor decision. While I was not involved in any inappropriate conduct at the Minneapolis airport or anywhere else, I chose to plead guilty to a lesser charge in the hope of making it go away. I did not seek any counsel, either from an attorney, staff, friends, or family. That was a mistake, and I deeply regret it. Because of that, I have now retained counsel and I am asking my counsel to review this matter and to advise me on how to proceed. For a moment, I want to put my state of mind into context on June 11. For eight months leading up to June, my family and I had been relentlessly and viciously harassed by the Idaho Statesman. If you've seen today's paper, you know why. Let me be clear: I am not gay and never have been." (08/28/07)
https://www.cnn.com/2007/POLITICS/08/28/sen.craig.statement/

"Fraud is in the culture of Iraqis. I believe that is true in the state of Louisiana as well." (10/18/05)
https://www.huffpost.com/entry/a-culture-of-fraud-where-_b_11734

Matt Gaetz

Congressman from FL 1st District since 2017

4 years in DC

"...this is a good time to be a fun-loving politician instead of a stick-in-the-mud." [And]" If politicians' family lives aren't what really matter to the voters, maybe that's a good thing. I'm a representative, not a monk." (09/14/21)
https://www.vanityfair.com/news/2020/09/matt-gaetz-donald-trump-firebrand

"Gaetz recalls another exchange with former congressman Jack Kingston, now a lobbyist, during his first year in Congress. 'Sure, the job only pays $172,000,' he writes Kingston told him. 'But with all the travel and fundraisers you get to do, it's more like a $400,000-$500,000 package. Take advantage of it!'" (09/14/21)
https://www.vanityfair.com/news/2020/09/matt-gaetz-donald-trump-firebrand

"Deal. I want Gaetzgate." [Replying to Elon Musk tweet stating, "If there's ever a scandal about me, *please* call it Elongate."] (03/25/21)
https://twitter.com/mattgaetz/status/1375094924882874375

"Well you know what? Silicon Valley can't cancel this movement, or this rally, or this Congressman. We have a Second Amendment in this country, and I think we have an obligation to use it." (05/28/21)
https://www.abcactionnews.com/news/state/florida-rep-gaetz-says-americans-have-obligation-to-use-2nd-amendment

"Now that we clearly see Antifa as terrorists, can we hunt them down like we do those in the Middle East?"
(06/01/2020) https://twitter.com/mattgaetz/status/1267513356853919744

"The media is painting Khashoggi as a "journalist" rather than a political participant. Don't get me wrong, I'm 100% opposed to killing people for their politics, but IDK that this is journalism." (10/17/2018)
https://twitter.com/mattgaetz/status/1052731209208537088

"Only God can judge. But we can sure set up the meeting." (04/29/13)
https://www.reuters.com/article/idUSBRE93S0UT20130429?irpc=932

"I think there are people that have some loose affiliation with the deep state that are out to get Jim Jordan." (07/12/18) https://thehill.com/homenews/house/396650-gop-lawmaker-accusations-against-jim-jordan-come-from-deep-state

"If that is a crime tell me when the prison sentence starts." [Openly violated House rule by renting office space below market value and not disclosing it.] (04/23/20)
https://www.pnj.com/story/news/2020/04/22/gaetz-merrill-subjects-common-cause-complaints-full-disclosure/3008376001/

John Kasich

Congressman from OH 12th District from 1983 - 2001

18 Years in DC

"I said, 'All of a sudden, you couldn't buy an AR-15, what would you lose? Would you feel as though your Second Amendment rights would be eroded because you couldn't buy a God-darn AR-15?' These are the things that have to be looked at." (02/18/18) https://www.nbcnews.com/politics/politics-news/gop-sen-lankford-open-stronger-gun-background-checks-n849176

"I don't need your people." [Said to black Ohio senator when she offered to help his cabinet. Meant Democrats but took to mean black people.] (01/28/11) https://www.politico.com/story/2011/01/ohio-gov-i-dont-need-your-people-048362

"If you're not on the bus, we'll run over you with the bus. And I'm not kidding." [Message to lobbyists that oppose him.] (07/21/15) https://www.latimes.com/nation/la-pn-kasich-2016-20150721-story.html#page=1

"I don't know about you, lady, but when I get to the pearly gates, I'm going to have an answer for what I've done for the poor." (06/19/15) https://www.politico.com/story/2015/06/john-kasich-replace-jeb-bush-2016-candidate-119191

"He's an idiot! We just can't act that way. What people resent are people who are in the government who don't treat the client with respect." [Called police officer an idiot for giving him a ticket for passing an emergency vehicle with its lights on.] (01/12/19) https://www.cleveland.com/open/2011/02/ohio_gov_john_kasich_calls_pol.html

Lindsey Graham

Congressman from SC 3rd District from 1995 - 2003

Senator from SC since 2003

26 years in DC

"Eating a taco is probably not gonna fix the problems we have with Hispanics. I think embracing Donald Trump is embracing demographic death." (05/11/16)
https://www.politico.com/story/2016/05/lindsey-graham-hispanics-donald-trump-223073

"If you killed Ted Cruz on the floor of the Senate, and the trial was in the Senate, nobody would convict you." (02/26/16) https://edition.cnn.com/2016/02/26/politics/lindsey-graham-ted-cruz-dinner/

"Everything I know about the Iranians I learned at the pool room. I met a lot of liars, and I know the Iranians are lying." (05/22/15) https://www.bbc.com/news/world-us-canada-32850481

"And here's the first thing I would do if I were president of the United States. I wouldn't let Congress leave town until we fix this. I would literally use the military to keep them in if I had to. We're not leaving town until we restore these defense cuts. We are not leaving town until we restore the intel cuts." (03/12/15) https://www.vox.com/2015/3/11/8193751/lindsey-graham-military-coup?__c=1

"Free speech is a great idea, but we're in a war." (04/03/11)
https://www.realclearpolitics.com/video/2011/04/03/lindsey_graham_free_speech_is_a_great_idea_but_were_in_a_war.html

"If you think he's a racist, that's up to you—I don't." [After calling Trump "a race-baiting, xenophobic religious bigot."] (07/18/19)
https://www.newsweek.com/lindsey-graham-trump-not-racist-tweets-1450060

"You know what concerns me about the American press is this endless, endless attempt to label the guy as some kind of kook not fit to be president. He did win, by the way. He beat me and 16 others." [Called Trump a "kook" in 2016.] (11/30/17)
https://ca.finance.yahoo.com/news/nobody-can-call-trump-kook-around-lindsey-graham-called-trump-kook-201136963.html

Mark Walker

Congressman from NC 6th District from 2015 - 2021

6 years in DC

"The accomplished men and women of the RSC. And women. If it wasn't sexist, I would say the RSC eye candy, but we'll leave that out of the record." (09/27/17)
https://www.cnn.com/2017/09/26/politics/mark-walker-eye-candy-remarks/index.html

"If it looks like a duck and walks like a duck, it must be government waste." [Criticizing duck ramp on the Capitol Reflecting Pool.] (05/15/17) https://twitter.com/RepMarkWalker/status/864223017135689728

"But I would tell you, if you have foreigners who are sneaking in with drug cartels, to me that is a national threat, and if we got to go laser or blitz somebody with a couple of fighter jets for a little while to make our point, I don't have a problem with that either." (09/18/14) https://www.wral.com/walker-he-doesn-t-have-a-qualm-about-war-with-mexico/13995217/

"For six decades, we have maintained at the centennial mark. Why not keep it 100?" [Regarding amendment to not expand Senate to limit any new states from having representation.] (10/02/20) https://thehill.com/blogs/congress-blog/politics/519283-want-to-prevent-democrat-destruction-save-our-senate

"China's lack of transparency created this. Now we are asking American taxpayers to foot the bill? Not hardly! I am working on a plan to make the Communist Party of China pay for this stimulus package. More to come soon." (03/26/20) https://twitter.com/RepMarkWalker/status/1243246178646609920

Tom DeLay

Congressman from TX 22nd District from 1985 - 2006
21 years in DC

"We've already found a secret memo coming out of the Justice Department. They're now going to go after 12 new perversions, things like bestiality, polygamy, having sex with little boys and making that legal. Not only that, but they have a whole list of strategies to go after the churches, the pastors, and any businesses that tries to assert their religious liberty. This is coming and it's coming like a tidal wave."
(06/30/15)
https://www.youtube.com/watch?v=GZy8V7NAagQ&ab_channel=NewsmaxTV

"If we had those 40 million children that were [aborted] over the last 30 years, we wouldn't need the illegal immigrants to fill the jobs that they are doing today."
(07/19/07)
https://www.youtube.com/watch?v=gFGit_tZDqs&ab_channel=MaxBlumenthal

"Now tell me the truth boys, is this kind of fun?" [Asked of Hurricane Katrina evacuee children while seeking refuge at Astrodome.]
(09/10/05) https://www.washingtonpost.com/wp-dyn/content/article/2005/09/09/AR2005090901930.html

"My friends, there is no Palestinian-Israeli conflict. There is only the global war on terrorism." (08/31/04)
http://www.nbcnews.com/id/5822374/ns/politics-tom_curry/t/delay-makes-intense-appealfor-jewish-voters/#.X2z4gmhKhPY

"Yes, I don't think that Newt could set a high moral standard, a high moral tone, during that moment. You can't do that if you're keeping secrets about your own adulterous affairs. [The difference between {my} own adultery and Gingrich's] is that I was no longer committing adultery by that time, the impeachment trial. There's a big difference. Also, I had returned to Christ and repented my sins by that time."
(05/28/07) https://www.newyorker.com/magazine/2007/06/04/party-unfaithful

Marjorie Taylor Greene

Congresswoman from GA 14th District since 2021
1 year in DC

"Vaccinated employees get a vaccination logo just like the Nazi's forced Jewish people to wear a gold star." (05/25/21)
https://twitter.com/mtgreenee/status/1397150992341377027

"You ran a Nov 3rd election that was stolen bc you idiots at the SOS mailed out millions of absentee ballots to anyone and everyone while GA was an open state." (01/17/21)
https://twitter.com/mtgreenee/status/1350812454918496257

[Holding AR - 15] "I have a message for Antifa terrorists - stay the hell out of northwest Georgia." [Cocks rifle.] (06/05/20)
https://patch.com/georgia/dallas-hiram/gop-house-candidate-warns-antifa-stay-hell-out-nw-ga

"Squad's worst nightmare" [Posted meme on Facebook of her wielding AR-15 next to OAC, Omar, and Tlaib.] (09/04/20)
https://www.buzzfeednews.com/article/juliareinstein/marjorie-taylor-greene-qanon-gun-facebook-squad

"[The question is] paranoid and ridiculous. Fake news is always looking for the next conspiracy theory. Go back to bed." (09/04/20)
https://www.forbes.com/sites/jackbrewster/2020/09/03/trump-backed-qanon-candidate-posts-meme-showing-off-gun-and-urging-offense-against-aoc-the-squad/?sh=75441ed96aca

"Trump won" [wore mask with "Trump won" written on front on the House floor on her first day in office.] (01/04/21)
https://thehill.com/homenews/532534-rep-elect-marjorie-taylor-greene-wears-trump-won-mask-on-house-floor

"President Trump will remain in office. This Hail Mary attempt to remove him from the White House is an attack on every American who voted for him. Democrats must be held accountable for the political violence inspired by their rhetoric." (01/12/21)
https://twitter.com/mtgreenee/status/1349190884592660488

"On January 21st, I'm filing Articles of Impeachment on President-elect @JoeBiden." (01/14/21)
https://twitter.com/mtgreenee/status/1349519602888355840

"She's a hypocrite. She's anti-American. And we're going to kick that bitch out of Congress." [Referring to Nancy Pelosi.] (08/12/20) https://www.foxnews.com/politics/gop-primary-winner-marjorie-taylor-greene-pelosi

"That's another one of those Clinton murders." [Referring to JFK, Jr. plane crash death in 1999.] (11/01/18)
https://www.youtube.com/watch?t=1850&v=jhe9Fd6YRyA&feature=youtu.be

"The idea is clean energy to replace coal and oil. If they are beaming the suns energy back to Earth, I'm sure they wouldn't ever miss a transmitter receiving station right??!! I mean mistakes are never made when anything new is invented. What would that look like anyway? A laser beam or light beam coming down to Earth I guess. Could that cause a fire?" (11/17/18) https://www.mediamatters.org/facebook/marjorie-taylor-greene-penned-conspiracy-theory-laser-beam-space-started-deadly-2018

Joe Scarborough

Congressman from FL 1st District from 1995 - 2001
6 years in DC

"A guy who had information that would have destroyed rich and powerful men's lives ends up dead in his jail cell. How predictably...Russian." (08/10/19)
https://www.theatlantic.com/politics/archive/2019/08/epstein-suicide-conspiracies/595906/

"My son, born in 1991, has a slight form of autism called Asperger`s. When I was practicing law and also when I was in Congress, parents would constantly come to me and they would bring me videotapes of their children, and they were all around the age of my son or younger. So, something happened in 1989." (06/22/05)
http://www.nbcnews.com/id/8243264/ns/msnbc-morning_joe/t/coverup-cause-autism/#.X3YWSmhKhPY

"I think it's safe to say, if you just look at the federal records, Mika, [Trump] is the least successful business person of all time." (11/28/20) https://www.yahoo.com/entertainment/joe-scarborough-blasts-trump-least-140845991.html

"Well, not conservatives. You can't be conservative and support Donald Trump. Trumpists are even saying that now." (04/15/20) https://www.foxnews.com/media/msnbcs-joe-scarborough-you-cant-be-conservative-and-support-donald-trump

"Right now, these conservatives are making Democrats, who are pro-choice, actually look more pro-life. Because they are only worried about the unborn. It is the born — it is the weakest among us, it is senior citizens — who they are ready to euthanize, because they want Boeing's corporate earnings to not dip too low." (03/26/20) https://www.salon.com/2020/03/26/joe-scarborough-democrats-look-more-pro-life-than-republicans-amid-calls-to-euthanize-elderly/

"[Trump is] full blown crazy. [The president has] got to be on something." (12/23/20)
https://www.forbes.com/sites/markjoyella/2020/12/23/msnbcs-joe-scarborough-on-new-trump-video-hes-got-to-be-on-something/?sh=af28eb12dfef

"You [Trump] really should have read the Constitution and a little bit of history before you got into office. I heard you had Mein Kampf by your bedside. I think your wife said you had Mein Kampf, your ex-wife said you had Mein Kampf by your bedside. Should have had the Constitution. It should have been a little bit of history, and you would understand that Supreme Court justices, they can't do what you're asking them to do." (12/14/20) https://www.newsweek.com/msnbcs-joe-scarborough-mocks-trump-heard-you-had-mein-kampf-bedside-shouldve-had-1554647

Bob Dornan

Congressman from CA 46th District from 1977 - 1997

20 years in DC

"I tend to trivialize the men (in the pro-choice movement). They're either women trapped in men's bodies, like Alan Alda and Phil Donahue, or younger guys who are like camp followers looking for easy lays. Those males don't vote. And when they do, they're starry-eyed liberal Democrats who subscribe to Playboy." (2/10/90) https://www.latimes.com/archives/la-xpm-1990-02-10-li-392-story.html

"It's the Year of the Penis." (01/28/94)
https://www.latimes.com/archives/la-xpm-1994-07-15-mn-15842-story.html

"You're a disgrace to your baptism. You're a poor excuse for a Marine. You're a pathetic, old, senile man. You're a slimy coward. Go register in another party." [Said about Republican attorney supporting Democratic candidate.] (11/18/96)
https://www.latimes.com/archives/la-xpm-1996-11-23-mn-8102-story.html

"I used to pine away that my birthday wasn't April 13th," he says. "That was Thomas Jefferson's birthday, and I loved Thomas Jefferson. I always wished I had a '1' in front of my '3' -- until I discovered that April 3rd was the day that Christ was crucified." (04/03/1985)
https://www.washingtonpost.com/archive/lifestyle/1985/04/04/bob-dornan-combat-ready/e68c21fe-5695-43ae-8853-462b0b4eec6f/

"I was born just a few weeks after Adolf Hitler came to power. Adolf Hitler was sworn in as Reichschancellor on FDR's birthday, the 30th of January -- which happens to be the day I joined the Air Force, too -- 30 January 1933. In those days we swore our president in on March the 4th. Roosevelt was sworn in March the 4th, and I was born 29 days later. So I was alive in my mother's womb when Hitler came to power." (04/04/1985)
https://www.washingtonpost.com/archive/lifestyle/1985/04/04/bob-dornan-combat-ready/e68c21fe-5695-43ae-8853-462b0b4eec6f/

"If he wants to get into veterinarian metaphors he should have been spayed, fixed when he was a young man and maybe he'd get a second term as President." [Regarding Bill Clinton.] (06/27/1995) https://www.nytimes.com/1995/06/27/us/appearing-nightly-robert-dornan-master-of-the-put-down.html

Spades

John Kerry

Senator from MA from 1985 - 2013
US Secretary of State from 2013 - 2017
Presidential Envoy for Climate since 2021
33 years in DC

"I actually did vote for the $87 billion before I voted against it." (09/30/04)
https://www.cnn.com/2004/ALLPOLITICS/09/30/kerry.comment/

"You know, education, if you make the most of it, you study hard, you do your homework and you make an effort to be smart, you can do well. If you don't, you get stuck in Iraq." (11/01/06)
http://www.nbcnews.com/id/15499174/ns/politics/t/uproar-over-kerry-iraq-remarks/#.X4zGrdBKhPY

"We're going to keep pounding. [The Bush administration] guys are the most crooked, you know, lying group I've ever seen. It's scary." (03/10/04)
http://www.nbcnews.com/id/4497642/ns/politics/t/bush-kerry-tradejabs-economy/#.X4zH9tBKhPY

"Somebody told me the other day that the Secret Service has orders that if George Bush is shot, they're to shoot Quayle." (11/17/88) https://www.latimes.com/archives/la-xpm-1988-11-17-mn-494-story.html

"When the president of the United States looks at you and tells you something, there should be some trust." [Blames President Bush for his voting in favor of Iraq war] (01/28/04)
https://www.cnn.com/2004/US/01/27/sprj.nirq.bush/

"Given this challenge we face today, and given the progress of fourth generation nuclear: go for it. No other alternative, zero emissions." (01/09/17)
https://www.wbur.org/bostonomix/2017/01/09/john-kerry-mit-climate-change

"Perhaps the media would do us all a service if they didn't cover [terrorism] quite as much. People wouldn't know what's going on." (08/30/16) https://www.businessinsider.com/john-kerry-media-terrorism-2016-8

"Now, I know there are still a few who insist that climate change is one big hoax, even a political conspiracy. My friends, these people are so out of touch with science that they believe rising sea levels don't matter, because, in their view, the extra water is just going to spill out over the sides of a flat Earth." (12/09/15)

https://www.democracynow.org/2015/12/9/it_is_not_enough_despite_promise

"There are all kinds of atrocities, and I would have to say that, yes, yes, I committed the same kind of atrocities as thousands of other soldiers have committed, in that I took part in shootings in free-fire zones, I conducted harassment and interdiction fire, I used .50-caliber machine guns which were granted and ordered to use, which were our only weapon against people. I took part in search-and-destroy missions, in the burning of villages." (04/22/71)

https://www.cnn.com/2004/ALLPOLITICS/04/25/hughes.kerry.vietnam/index.html

Alexandria Ocasio-Cortez

Congresswoman from NY 14th District since 2019

2 years in DC

"Millennials and people, you know, Gen Z and all these folks that will come after us are looking up and we're like: The world is going to end in 12 years if we don't address climate change and your biggest issue is how are we gonna pay for it? And, like, this is the war – this is our World War 2." (01/21/19)
https://www.youtube.com/watch?v=oHk8nn0nw18&t=9s&ab_channel=TheDCShorts

"Dems are burning precious time & impact negotiating w/GOP." (06/09/21) https://twitter.com/AOC/status/1402699406202245127

"GOP defensively say, 'we're not scared of dancing women!' yet proceed to use footage of me dancing 'with the color drained to make it look more ominous.' 🤭 Spoiler: The GOP *is* scared of dancing women, because they fear the liberation of all identities taught to feel shame." (02/28/19)
https://twitter.com/aoc/status/1101166967787012097?lang=en

"If you're mad that I think people SHOULD KNOW when Dems vote to expand ICE powers, then be mad. ICE is a dangerous agency with 0 accountability, widespread reporting of rape, abuse of power, + children dying in DHS custody. Having a D next to your name doesn't make that right." (03/02/19) https://twitter.com/AOC/status/1101835308704952320

"Members of Congress have a duty to respond to the President's explicit attack today. @IlhanMN's life is in danger. For our colleagues to be silent is to be complicit in the outright, dangerous targeting of a member of Congress. We must speak out." (04/12/19)
https://twitter.com/AOC/status/1116848329776934912

"So we talk about existential threats, the last time we had a really major existential threat to this country was around World War II. And so we've been here before and we have a blueprint of doing this before. None of these things are new ideas. What we had was an existential threat in the context of a war. We had a direct existential threat with another nation, this time it was Nazi Germany, and the Axis, who explicitly made the United States as an enemy, as an enemy. What we did was that we chose to mobilize our entire economy and industrialized our entire economy and we put hundreds of thousands if not millions of people to work in defending our shores and defending this country. We have to do the same thing in order to get us to 100 percent renewable energy, and that's just the truth of it." (10/19/18)
https://www.youtube.com/watch?v=PKeTDN8PiBc

"So the whole "progressivism is bad" argument just doesn't have any compelling evidence that I've seen. When it comes to "Defund" & "Socialism" attacks, people need to realize these are racial resentment attacks. You're not gonna make that go away. You can make it less effective." (11/06/20)
https://twitter.com/AOC/status/1324698828944138243

Amy Klobuchar

Senator from MN since 2007

14 years in DC

"I have won every place, every race — every time I've won." (07/15/19)
https://www.mprnews.org/story/2019/07/14/klobuchar-sharpens-electability-message

"The people pick the President; the President nominates the Justice. That is how it works." [Contradicting her opposition to late term appointment by President Trump to Supreme Court.] (09/21/20)
https://twitter.com/amyklobuchar/status/1308149561240813569

"For me, whatever happened before, ancient rules, whatever it is, what matters right now is that they just made these statements. They're not beholden to Mitch McConnell. They're beholden to the people that voted for them in their own state. So if my colleagues want to look themselves in the mirror and say, 'What did I just say the last time this happened? What's the precedent I set? What should I follow?' They each have to make an individual decision." (09/20/20)
https://www.msn.com/en-us/news/politics/amy-klobuchar-dodges-question-about-senate-precedent-for-confirming-justices-during-election-year/ar-BB19esby

"This is a historic moment, and America must seize on this moment. And I truly believe as, I actually told the vice president last night when I called him, that I think this is a moment to put a woman of color on that ticket." (06/19/20)
https://www.cnn.com/2020/06/18/politics/biden-vice-president-amy-klobuchar/index.html

"...if you think a woman can't beat Donald Trump, Nancy Pelosi does it every single day." (11/21/19)
https://www.cnn.com/2019/11/20/politics/amy-klobuchar-woman-trump-nancy-pelosi-debate/index.html

"Well, I'm hoping I get to dance with you in that outfit. I'm thinking at the end of the interview." (11/6/19) https://www.nytimes.com/2019/11/06/us/amy-klobuchar-comedy.html

"So I wrote back - 'Hey Donald Trump, the science is on my side and I'd like to see how your hair would fare in a blizzard.'" [Told same attempted joke repeatedly.] (09/05/19) https://twitter.com/TheDailyShow/status/1169777484113444864

"This wasn't meddling. That's what I do when I call my daughter on a Saturday night and ask her what she's doing. Sorry. This was much more serious than that. This was actually invading our election." (10/15/19) https://www.washingtonpost.com/politics/2019/10/15/october-democratic-debate-transcript/

Harry Reid

Congressman from NV 1ˢᵗ District from 1983 - 1987

Senator from NV 1987 - 2017

34 years in DC

"[Obama is a] light-skinned African American with no Negro dialect, unless he wanted to have one." (01/09/10)
https://www.cnn.com/2010/POLITICS/01/09/obama.reid/index.html

"You think you've heard these same excuses before? You're right. In this country there were those who dug in their heels and said, 'Slow down, it's too early. Let's wait. Things aren't bad enough' — about slavery. When women wanted to vote [they said] 'Slow down, there will be a better day to do that — the day isn't quite right'..." [Regarding health care reform.] (12/07/09)
https://nymag.com/intelligencer/2009/12/harry_reid_thinks_health_care.html

"This confusing mix helps hide the fact that Members and most Federal employees, including the Congressional staffers, enjoy this generous mix of retirement benefits, which far exceed the benefits for the average American taxpayer. Median private pensions and annuities in 2019 was only $10,788, and only one-third of older Americans even receive pensions" to now say "This confusing mix helps hide the fact that Members and most Federal employees, including the Congressional staffers, enjoy this generous mix of retirement benefits, which far exceed the benefits for the average American taxpayer. Only 8 percent of private sector workers have the more desirable defined benefit retirement plans and only 47 percent have access to the more common contributory plans."
https://www.bls.gov/ncs/cbs/benefits/2018/ownership/private/table01a.pdf

"The man's father is a wonderful human being. I think this guy [George W. Bush] is a loser." (05/07/05)
https://www.washingtonpost.com/archive/politics/2005/05/07/reid-calls-bush-a-loser/44a0829b-72a5-42c0-96d7-fae65240810d/

Rolling Stone: "You've called Bush a loser."

Reid: "And a liar."

Rolling Stone: "You apologized for the loser comment."

Reid: "But never for the liar, have I?"

(06/16/05) https://www.rollingstone.com/politics/politics-news/harry-reid-the-gunslinger-191299/

"I know procedures around here. And I know that there will still be Senate business conducted. But I will, for lack of a better word, screw things up." (12/13/04)
https://www.washingtonpost.com/wp-dyn/articles/A59877-2004Dec12.html

"You son of a bitch, you tried to bribe me!" [While choking man who attempted to bribe him during FBI sting operation.] (05/30/06)
https://prospect.org/article/harry-reid-bribe-video/

"I don't know how anyone of Hispanic heritage could be a Republican, OK. Do I need to say more?" (08/11/10)
https://thehill.com/blogs/ballot-box/senate-races/113687-reid-i-dont-know-how-anyone-of-hispanic-heritage-can-be-a-republican

"Harry, he didn't pay any taxes for 10 years. He didn't pay taxes for 10 years! Now, do I know that that's true? Well, I'm not certain." (07/31/12) https://www.huffpost.com/entry/harry-reid-romney-taxes_n_1724027

"Romney didn't win, did he?" (03/31/15)
https://www.washingtonpost.com/news/the-fix/wp/2015/03/31/harry-reids-appalling-defense-of-his-attack-on-mitt-romneys-tax-record/

"It's too bad that they are trying to buy America. And it's time that the American people spoke out against this terrible dishonesty of these two [Koch] brothers, who are about as un-American as anyone that I can imagine." (02/16/14)
https://www.seattletimes.com/seattle-news/politics/harry-reid-koch-brothers-are-un-american/

Elizabeth Warren

Senator from MA since 2013
8 years in DC

"Donald Trump is a loud, nasty, thin-skinned fraud who has never risked anything for anyone and who serves no one but himself, and that is just one of the many reasons he will never be president of the United States, unfortunately just like Hillary Clinton." (06/09/16)
https://theweek.com/speedreads/629183/elizabeth-warren-lashes-donald-trump-thinskinned-racist-bully

"What's happening right now in cryptocurrency, like Bitcoin and Dogecoin, it's a Wild West out there." (06/09/21)
https://twitter.com/BloombergTV/status/1402749016845262851

"There is nobody in this country who got rich on his own — nobody. You built a factory out there? Good for you. But I want to be clear. You moved your goods to market on the roads the rest of us paid for." (09/21/12)
https://www.cbsnews.com/news/elizabeth-warren-there-is-nobody-in-this-country-who-got-rich-on-his-own/

"At best you were incompetent, at worst you were complicit." [Speaking to former Wells Fargo CEO.] (10/03/17)
https://www.bostonglobe.com/news/politics/2017/10/03/wells-fargo-ceo-faces-angry-warren-congress/t5FRqFfFrqZaOEbxbRclyN/story.html

"Let's be honest - @realDonaldTrump is a loser. Count all his failed businesses. See how he cheated people w/ scams like Trump U." (03/21/16)
https://twitter.com/ewarren/status/711950372051558400

"@RealDonaldTrump knows he's a loser. His insecurities are on parade: petty bullying, attacks on women, cheap racism, flagrant narcissism." (03/21/16)
https://twitter.com/ewarren/status/711950735798304768

"Many of history's worst authoritarians started out as losers – and @realDonaldTrump is a serious threat." (03/21/16)
https://twitter.com/ewarren/status/711951101524840448

"The way I see it, it's our job to make sure @realDonaldTrump ends this campaign every bit the loser that he started it." (03/21/16)
https://twitter.com/ewarren/status/711951221490372609

"Being Native American is part of who our family is and I'm glad to tell anyone about that. I am just very proud of it." [Failed DNA test.] (05/03/12) https://www.cbsnews.com/news/warren-explains-minority-listing-talks-of-grandfathers-high-cheekbones/

"Race: American Indian" [Listing race on her state bar registration.] (04/18/96)
https://twitter.com/AmyEGardner/status/1092941590555971585

Hillary Clinton

Senator from NY 2001 – 2009

Secretary of State from 2009 – 2013

12 years in DC

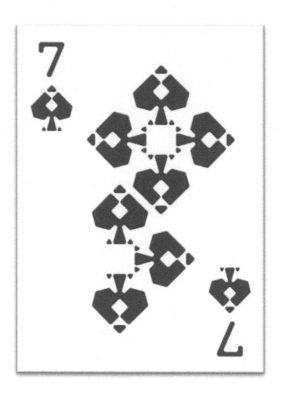

"But with all due respect, the fact is we had four dead Americans. Was it because of a protest, or was it because of guys out for a walk one night who decided they'd go kill some Americans? What difference, at this point, does it make?" (01/23/13) https://www.bbc.com/news/21161346

"I could have told him [Putin] he was a KGB agent by definition he doesn't have a soul. I mean this is a waste of time, right?" (08/24/18)
http://transcripts.cnn.com/TRANSCRIPTS/1808/24/csr.01.html

"Well, Tom, I can tell you that I may be a lot of things, but I'm not dumb. And I wrote about going to Bosnia in my book in 2004. I laid it all out there. And you're right. On a couple of occasions in the last weeks I just said some things that weren't in keeping with what I knew to be the case and what I had written about in my book. And, you know, I'm embarrassed by it. I have apologized for it. I've said it was a mistake. And it is, I hope, something that you can look over, because clearly I am proud that I went to Bosnia. It was a war zone." (04/17/08) https://www.chicagotribune.com/chinews-mtblog-2008-04-clinton_admits_lying_about_bos-story.html

"When (Republicans) talk about legal (immigration) status, that's code for second-class status." (05/05/15)
https://www.c-span.org/video/?c4537190/user-clip-i5515i-hillary-code-class-status

"As president, I will take steps to ban the box, so former presidents won't have to declare their criminal history at the very start of the hiring process." (11/04/15)
https://www.theatlantic.com/notes/2015/11/gaffe-track-hillarys-freudian-slip-on-prisoners-and-presidents/414130/

"Women have always been the primary victims of war. Women lose their husbands, their fathers, their sons in combat." (11/17/98)
https://web.archive.org/web/20010726225357/http://clinton3.nara.gov/WH/EOP/First_Lady/html/generalspeeches/1998/19981117.html

"He ran a gas station down in St. Louis. No, Mahatma Gandhi was a great leader of the 20th century." [Attempted joke.] (0/24/04)
http://web.archive.org/web/20051027070231/http://www.iht.com/articles/2004/01/21/edtripathi_ed3_.php#

"Many of you are well enough off that [President Bush's] tax cuts may have helped you. We're saying that for America to get back on track, we're probably going to cut that short and not give it to you. We're going to have to take things away from you on behalf of the common good." (08/25/07)
https://abcnews.go.com/Politics/story?id=3523981&page=1

"I have a million ideas. The country can't afford them all." (10/11/07)
http://archive.boston.com/news/nation/articles/2007/10/11/clinton_vows_to_check_executive_power/

Max Baucus

Congressman from MT 1st District from 1975 - 1978

Senator from MT from 1978 - 2014

US Ambassador to China from 2014 - 2017

42 years in DC

"This is not rocket science. Here's what really concerns me, the administration rhetoric is so strong against China it's over the top. We are entering kind of an era which is similar to Joe McCarthy back when he was red-baiting [the] State Department in attacking communism [and] a little bit like Hitler in the 30s in that a lot of people knew what was going on was wrong, they knew it was wrong, but they didn't stand up and say anything about it, they felt intimidated." (05/06/20)
https://www.dailywire.com/news/obama-biden-ambassador-to-china-china-bashing-over-coronavirus-like-hitler-in-the-30s

"I think that the big lesson here [is] that when you take charge and when you tell the entire country, Wuhan, other provinces what to do, they get in gear and get the job done. I take my hat off to China for doing so." (03/24/20)
https://freebeacon.com/national-security/i-take-my-hat-off-to-china-obamas-china-ambassador-praises-chinese-response-to-virus/

"I think the U.S. has been hypercritical of China ... sometimes without any proof. This is a political season in the U.S., and politicians are using China as a scapegoat to help them get elected." (07/29/20) https://freebeacon.com/national-security/dem-max-baucus-attacks-china-critics-on-chinese-state-tv/

"The Chinese are so tough, they can withstand more pain, in my judgment, than can Americans. The Chinese respect strength more than any other people. ... I think they can smell weakness better than any other people." (08/13/19)
https://www.cnbc.com/2019/08/13/amb-max-baucus-china-can-endure-more-pain-than-america.html

"I'm no real expert on China." (0/31/14)
https://www.washingtonpost.com/blogs/in-the-loop/wp/2014/01/31/presumptive-ambassador-to-china-baucus-im-no-real-expert-on-china/

"I'm a very proud Democrat, but I also like results."

(04/08/13) https://www.washingtonpost.com/business/economy/sen-max-baucus-moves-to-reshape-tax-code/2013/04/08/e7f3435a-9dff-11e2-9a79-eb5280c81c63_story.html

Rashida Tlaib

Congresswoman from MI 13th District since 2019
2 years in DC

"They forgot what country they represent." [Regarding Jewish Congress members, for supporting Israel.] (01/6/19) https://apnews.com/article/6e38e4e5f6f8a228058aad8665722f57

"Policing in our country is inherently & intentionally racist... No more policing, incarceration, and militarization. It can't be reformed." (04/12/21) https://twitter.com/RashidaTlaib/status/1381745303997534216

"There's kind of a calming feeling I always tell folks when I think of the Holocaust, and the tragedy of the Holocaust, and the fact that it was my ancestors, Palestinians, who lost their land and some lost their lives, their livelihood, their human dignity, their existence in many ways, have been wiped out, and some people's passports." (05/10/19) https://www.rollcall.com/2019/05/13/rep-rashida-tlaib-defends-holocaust-israel-comments-against-critics/

"'Look, Mama, you won. Bullies don't win,'" Tlaib said. "And I said, 'Baby, they don't, because we're gonna go in there and impeach the motherf---er.'" [Claims conversation with her son.] (01/03/19) https://www.newsweek.com/congresswoman-rashida-tliab-refers-donald-trump-speech-tells-crowd-democrats-1279078

"Look, it's not a waste of time to hold the President United States accountable. We need to understand our duties as members of Congress and I believe looking at even Nixon's impeachment, it was Republicans and Democrats coming together and putting country first." (01/17/19) https://theintercept.com/2019/01/17/when-do-we-impeach-the-motherfucker-with-rashida-tlaib/

"We must be equitable in our outrage. We must abolish ICE." (06/24/19) https://www.metrotimes.com/news-hits/archives/2019/06/24/tlaib-deny-ice-its-request-for-more-funding-abolish-it

"These attacks are fundamentally led by white men in government who have no legal or moral authority to control our bodies, and who would surely revolt if women legislators proposed, for instance, mandatory vasectomies for all men in this country." (05/21/19) https://www.pressandguide.com/news/tlaib-slams-draconian-dangerous-anti-abortion-bills/article_db61981c-7b7a-11e9-9768-f7914c532fc5.html

"Sometimes I say, 'Thank her,' because my Allah is She." (08/14/18) https://www.nytimes.com/2018/08/14/us/politics/rashida-tlaib-muslim-congress.html

Chris Murphy

Congressman from CT 5th District from 2007 - 2013

Senator from CT since 2013

14 years in DC

"Since Sandy Hook there has been a school shooting, on average, every week. How on earth can we live with ourselves if we do nothing?" (06/24/15)
https://www.washingtonpost.com/news/fact-checker/wp/2015/06/29/has-there-been-one-school-shooting-per-week-since-sandy-hook/

"Your "thoughts" should be about steps to take to stop this carnage. Your "prayers" should be for forgiveness if you do nothing - again." (12/02/15)
https://twitter.com/ChrisMurphyCT/status/672176555859296256

"[Donors] have fundamentally different problems than other people, and in Connecticut especially, you spend a lot of time on the phone with people who work in the financial markets. And so you're hearing a lot about problems that bankers have and not a lot of problems that people who work at the mill in Thomaston, Conn., have. You certainly have to stop and check yourself." (05/07/13)
https://www.huffpost.com/entry/chris-murphy-fundraising_n_3232143

"My truth hierarchy: (1) health care is a human right (2) climate change is an existential threat (3) the Yankees suck." (04/03/17)
https://twitter.com/ChrisMurphyCT/status/848874949586636800

"@realDonaldTrump about to take stage at NRA, to celebrate right of criminals to own guns, to glorify weapons that kill." (04/28/17)
https://twitter.com/ChrisMurphyCT/status/858013387900497921

"I wanted to show some of the faces of Washington's inaction — to share a small sliver of the lives we've lost because our nation is overflowing with guns." (04/28/17)
https://www.nytimes.com/2017/04/28/us/politics/christopher-murphy-guns-trump.html?_r=0

"The paralysis you feel right now — the impotent helplessness that washes over you as news of another mass slaughter scrolls across the television screen — isn't real. It's a fiction created and methodically cultivated by the gun lobby, designed to assure that no laws are passed to make America safer, because those laws would cut into their profits."
(11/05/17) https://www.businessinsider.com/chris-murphy-texas-church-shooting-sutherland-springs-2017-11

Jerry Nadler

Congressman from NY 10th District since 1992

29 years in DC

"Nine-eleven was an act of war. The villains aren't the terrorists. The villains live in the White House." (03/06/07)
https://www.nytimes.com/2007/03/06/us/politics/06hillary.html

"Filling the SCOTUS vacancy during a lame duck session, after the American people have voted for new leadership, is undemocratic and a clear violation of the public trust in elected officials. Congress would have to act and expanding the court would be the right place to start." (11/19/20) https://www.businessinsider.com/jerry-nadler-house-judiciary-democrats-republicans-ginsburg-supreme-court-expansion-2020-9

"That's a myth that's being spread only in Washington DC." [Denying Antifa violence.] (07/26/20) https://nypost.com/2020/07/27/jerry-nadler-calls-violence-from-antifa-in-portland-a-myth/

"There must never be a narrowly voted impeachment or an impeachment substantially supported by one of our major political parties and largely opposed by the other. Such an impeachment would lack legitimacy, would produce divisiveness and bitterness in our politics for years to come and will call into question the very legitimacy of our political institutions." (12/10/98) https://www.nbcnews.com/politics/trump-impeachment-inquiry/flashback-what-nadler-said-about-impeaching-president-1998-n1095141

"Paper ballots are extremely susceptible to fraud. And at least with the old clunky voting machines that we have in New York, the deliberate fraud is way down compared to paper. When the machines break down, they vote on paper – they've had real problems." [Now supports mail- in ballots.] (12/08/2004) https://nypost.com/2020/05/27/jerry-nadler-warned-of-possible-paper-ballot-fraud-in-2004/

Dianne Feinstein

Senator from CA since 1992
29 years in DC

"Several years ago I changed my view of the death penalty. It became crystal clear to me that the risk of unequal application is high and its effect on deterrence is low." (05/23/18) https://www.mercurynews.com/2018/05/23/when-did-dianne-feinstein-start-opposing-the-death-penalty/

"I sometimes say that in my last life maybe I was Chinese." (03/22/96) https://www.latimes.com/archives/la-xpm-1996-03-22-mn-50059-story.html

"The problem with expanding this is that, you know, with the advent of PTSD, which I think is a new phenomenon as a product of the Iraq War, it's not clear how the seller or transferrer of a firearm covered by this bill would verify that an individual was a member, or a veteran, and that there was no impairment of that individual with respect to having a weapon like this." (03/07/13) https://www.c-span.org/video/?311364-1/gun-control-legislation-markup

"Wearing masks in public should be mandatory. Period." [Seen in an airport without a mask.] (04/16/20) https://www.axios.com/dianne-feinstein-state-relief-funds-mask-mandate-092c10fc-900b-4629-b7a3-e176723d5add.html?utm_source=twitter&utm_medium=social&utm_campaign=organic&utm_content=1100

"And I think in your case, professor [Amy Barrett], when you read your speeches, the conclusion one draws is that the dogma lives loudly within you, and that's of concern when you come to big issues that large numbers of people have fought for years in this country." (09/07/17) https://www.washingtonpost.com/news/the-fix/wp/2017/09/07/did-a-democratic-senator-just-accuse-a-judicial-nominee-of-being-too-christian/

"I don't look at this as being a whistleblower. I think it's an act of treason." (06/10/13) https://thehill.com/policy/defense/304573-sen-feinstein-snowdens-leaks-are-treason

Chuck Schumer

Senator from NY since 1999

22 years in DC

"I want to tell you, Gorsuch. I want to tell you, Kavanaugh. You have released the whirlwind, and you will pay the price." (03/04/20) https://www.nationalreview.com/news/schumer-claims-conservative-supreme-court-justices-will-pay-the-price-if-they-rule-against-abortion-advocates/

"There is no inalienable right to own and operate 100-round clips on AR-15 assault rifles." (01/24/13) https://www.politico.com/story/2013/01/dianne-feinstein-assault-weapons-ban-086684

"...you have to force [Palestine] to say Israel is here to stay."

"...when there's some moderation and cooperation, [Palestine] can have an economic advancement."

"[Israel needs] to strangle them economically until they see that's not the way to go, makes sense"

(06/11/10) https://www.huffpost.com/entry/chuck-schumer-on-gaza-str_n_609594

"We have three branches of government. We have a House, we have a Senate, we have a President. And all three of us are gonna have to come together." (02/03/11) https://www.theatlantic.com/politics/archive/2011/02/video-how-come-we-didn-t-all-make-fun-of-chuck-schumer/342373/

"I don't know why they make [Tide Pods] look so delicious... I saw one on my staffer's desk and I wanted to eat it." (09/09/12) https://www.nydailynews.com/new-york/schumer-newfangled-detergent-pods-candy-article-1.1155442

"Senators will have to decide if Donald John Trump incited the erection." (01/22/21) https://dailycaller.com/2021/01/22/schumer-senators-have-to-decide-if-trump-incited-erection/

Adam Schiff

Congressman from CA 28th (AKA 27th and 29th)
District since 2001
20 years in DC

"The allegation that the President of the United States may have suborned perjury before our committee in an effort to curtail the investigation and cover up his business dealings with Russia is among the most serious to date. We will do what's necessary to find out if it's true." (01/19/19)
www.nbcnews.com/news/amp/ncna960156

I say this to the President, and his defenders in Congress: You may think it's okay how Trump and his associates interacted with Russians during the campaign. I don't. I think it's immoral. I think it's unpatriotic. And yes, I think it's corrupt." (03/28/19)
https://twitter.com/RepAdamSchiff/status/1111289977143545856?s=19

"I hear what you want. I have a favor I want from you, though. And I'm going to say this only seven times, so you better listen good. I want you to make up dirt on my political opponent. Understand? Lots of it, on this and on that."
[Pretending to be Trump] (09/27/19)
https://www.cnn.com/2019/09/27/politics/fact-check-adam-schiff-trumps-ukraine-call/index.html

"CBS News reported last night that a Trump confidant said that key senators were warned, 'Vote against the president and your head will be on a pike.' I don't know if that's true." (01/25/20) https://www.nbcnews.com/politics/2020-election/gop-senators-incensed-schiff-head-pike-remark-impeachment-trial-n1122761

"Concealing the truth is concealing Russians are again intervening to help the president in his reelection." (08/30/20)
https://www.foxnews.com/politics/russia-accusations-resurface-director-national-intelligence-election-security-briefings

"For precisely this reason, the president's misconduct cannot be decided at the ballot box — for we cannot be assured that the vote will be fairly won." (01/29/20)
https://www.rollcall.com/2020/01/29/adam-schiff-throws-the-ballot-box-under-the-bus/

"... yes, there's ample evidence of collusion in plain sight..." (04/07/19) https://www.newsweek.com/adam-schiff-tells-cnns-tapper-theres-ample-evidence-collusion-plain-sight-1388400

Hearts

Mo Brooks

Congressman from AL 5th District since 2011
10 years in DC

"What the Democrats are doing with their dividing America by race is they are waging a war on whites and I find that repugnant." (08/04/14)
https://www.politico.com/story/2014/08/mo-brooks-war-on-whites-109703

"Now, you want to talk about the problems associated with the Great Depression? They're a cakewalk compared to what can happen to our country if we don't start acting responsibly in Washington, D.C., to try to get this deficit under control." (09/17/11)
https://www.al.com/breaking/2011/09/mo_brooks.html

"Every time you have that soil or rock or whatever it is that is deposited into the seas, that forces the sea levels to rise, because now you have less space in those oceans, because the bottom is moving up." (05/17/18)
https://www.sciencemag.org/news/2018/05/republican-lawmaker-rocks-tumbling-ocean-causing-sea-level-rise

"These [DREAMERS] have to be absolutely 100 percent loyal and trustworthy, as best as we can make them, 'cause they're gonna have access to all sorts of military weaponry — even to the point of having access to weapons of mass destruction like our nuclear arsenal." (08/5/14) https://thehill.com/blogs/blog-briefing-room/news/214336-gop-lawmaker-dreamers-shouldnt-be-allowed-in-military-because

"A big lie is a political propaganda technique made famous by Germany's national socialist German Worker's Party. For more than two years, socialist Democrats and their fake news media allies, CNN, MSNBC, The New York Times, Washington Post and countless others, have perpetrated the biggest political lie, con, scam and fraud in American history." [Equates the Democratic party to the Nazi party after reading a page from Mein Kampf on the house floor.] (03/27/19)
https://www.usatoday.com/story/news/politics/2019/03/26/alabama-mo-brooks-quotes-hitler-house-floor-bash-democrats/3282595002/

"Today is the day American patriots start taking down names and kicking ass." [Said at Trump rally.] (01/06/21)
https://www.al.com/news/2021/01/mo-brooks-today-patriots-start-kicking-ass-in-fighting-vote-results.html

"Please, don't be like #FakeNewsMedia, don't rush to judgment on assault on Capitol. Wait for investigation. All may not be (and likely is not) what appears. Evidence growing that fascist ANTIFA orchestrated Capitol attack with clever mob control tactics." (01/07/21)
https://twitter.com/RepMoBrooks/status/1347171347043115008

Don Young

Congressman from AK since 1973

48 years in DC

"You know, I rarely do this, but I'm deeply disappointed in my good lady from Washington. (She) doesn't know a damn thing what she's talking about." (09/08/17)
https://edition.cnn.com/2017/09/08/politics/congressman-don-young-pramila-jayapal/index.html

"You want my money, my money... those [Republicans] who bite me will be bitten back." (07/19/07)
https://www.politico.com/blogs/politico-now/2007/07/north-to-alaska-002250

"My father had a ranch; we used to have 50-60 wetbacks to pick tomatoes." (03/29/13)
https://www.huffpost.com/entry/don-young-wetbacks_n_2976351?ref=topbar

Young: "and the, I call it garbage, Dr. Rice, that comes from the mouth —"

Brinkley: "Dr. Brinkley. Rice is a university." Young: "I'll say anything I want to say! You just be quiet!"

(11/18/11) https://www.washingtonpost.com/blogs/reliable-source/post/douglas-brinkley-and-rep-don-young-in-committee-hearing-smackdown/2011/11/18/gIQABxqVZN_blog.html

"Well, what, do you just go to the doctor and get diagnosed with suicide?" [Speaking to high school students after a student recently committed suicide.] "That boy needs to learn some respect." [Said about friend of victim that interrupted him] (10/22/14)
https://www.washingtonpost.com/news/the-fix/wp/2014/10/22/don-young-would-make-a-lousy-grief-counselor/

"There you go." [Head butts reporter's camera.] (10/31/19)
https://twitter.com/MoveOn/status/1189970650045263873

"[Environmentalists are] the self-centered bunch, the waffle-stomping, Harvard-graduating, intellectual bunch of idiots that don't understand that they're leading this country into environmental disaster." (1994) https://about.bgov.com/news/tell-it-like-it-is-rep-don-young-making-congressional-history/

"This suicide problem didn't exist until we got largesse from the government." (10/23/14)
https://www.politico.com/story/2014/10/don-young-suicide-government-handouts-112131

"[The BP oil spill] is not an environmental disaster, and I will say that again and again because it is a natural phenomenon. Oil has seeped into this ocean for centuries, will continue to do it. During World War II there was over 10 million barrels of oil spilt from ships, and no natural catastrophe. ... We will lose some birds, we will lose some fixed sealife, but overall it will recover." (05/23/11)
https://www.huffpost.com/entry/don-young-gulf-oil-spill-environmental-disaster_n_599392

Newt Gingrich

Congressman from GA 6th District from 1979 - 1999

20 years in DC

"75 years ago the Japanese displayed professional brilliance and technological power launching surprises from Hawaii to the Philippines." [Pearl Harbor Remembrance.] (12/07/16)
https://twitter.com/newtgingrich/status/806620424796860418

"She's not young enough or pretty enough to be the wife of the President. And besides, she has cancer." (reported 12/25/94) https://www.latimes.com/archives/la-xpm-1994-12-25-op-12904-story.html

"To take an ex-wife and make it two days before the primary a significant question in a presidential campaign is as close to despicable as anything I can imagine." [Denies asking his wife for an open marriage.] (01/20/12)
https://www.cnn.com/2012/01/19/politics/gop-debate/index.html

"A vicious lie. ... It is completely false." [Denies asking his wife to sign divorce papers when she was in a hospital bed recovering from cancer surgery, his daughters were eyewitnesses.] (12/10/11)
https://www.jacksonville.com/article/20111210/NEWS/801239733

"There's no question at times of my life, partially driven by how passionately I felt about this country, that I worked far too hard and things happened in my life that were not appropriate." [Excuse for infidelity.] (03/09/11)
https://web.archive.org/web/20110405185405/http://www.chicagotribune.com/news/sns-ap-us-newt-gingrich-2012%2C0%2C624356.story

"And I think that one of the great problems we have in the Republican Party is that we don't encourage you to be nasty." (06/24/78)
https://www.pbs.org/wgbh/pages/frontline/newt/newt78speech.html

"The idea that a congressman would be tainted by accepting money from private industry or private sources is essentially a socialist argument." (P. 31, October 1989)
https://books.google.com/books?id=EecDAAAAMBAJ&pg=PA30#v=onepage&q&f=false

"**1994**. People like me are what stand between us and Auschwitz. I see evil all around me every day." (04/07/11)
https://www.motherjones.com/politics/2011/04/newt-gingrich-greatest-rhetorical-hits/

"If you import a commercial quantity of illegal drugs, it is because you have made the personal decision that you are prepared to get rich by destroying our children. I have made the decision that I love our children enough that we will kill you if you do this." (08/27/95)
https://www.nytimes.com/1995/08/27/us/gingrich-suggests-tough-drug-measure.html

Glenn Grothman

Congressman from WI 6th District since 2015
6 years in DC

"Why sit down with 7th graders and say to some you will be heterosexual, some homosexual? Part of that agenda which is left unsaid is that some of those who throw it out as an option would like it if more kids became homosexuals." (02/11/10)
https://madison.com/ct/news/local/health_med_fit/vital_signs/article_f0ca35e4-1737-11df-b146-001cc4c03286.html

"I mean, what must God think of our country if now ... rather than sending people to Uganda to explain better agricultural techniques, sending missionaries to Africa, educating people on Christianity, we send scientists to Africa to say how wonderful the homosexual lifestyle is? It is just unbelievable what has become of our country." (04/30/14)
https://madison.com/news/local/writers/steven_elbow/glenn-grothman-blasts-u-s-moves-against-draconian-ugandan-homosexuality/article_ea072139-28d3-5019-be2e-13dd01e83029.html

"[Giving public employees [MLK] day off] is an insult to all the other taxpayers around the state." (05/22/12)
https://madison.com/wsj/news/local/govt-and-politics/blog/article_0ae9979a-2267-11e0-8190-001cc4c03286.html

"Of course, almost no black people today care about Kwanzaa - just white left-wingers who try to shove this down black people's throats in an effort to divide Americans... It's time it's slapped down once and for all." (12/28/12)
https://web.archive.org/web/20130124004244/http://thewheelerreport.com/wheeler_docs/files/1231grothman.pdf

"You could argue that money is more important for men. I think a guy in their first job, maybe because they expect to be a breadwinner someday, may be a little more money-conscious. To attribute everything to a so-called bias in the workplace is just not true." (05/22/12)
https://madison.com/ct/news/local/crime_and_courts/blog/crime-and-courts-sen-grothman-says-money-is-more-important/article_a8cb3254-831c-11e1-a4fc-0019bb2963f4.html

"[These protestors] are slobs. But I don't hate these people for being slobs. I don't mind nice slobs." (03/02/11)

https://madison.com/wsj/news/local/govt-and-politics/grothman-says-confrontation-with-protesters-didnt-scare-him/article_970dc490-44ee-11e0-855c-001cc4c03286.html

"Left and the social welfare establishment want children born out of wedlock because they are far more likely to be dependent on the government." (03/07/12)

https://chicagoist.com/2012/03/07/wi_grothman_parenthood_abuse.php

Ted Cruz

Senator from TX since 2013

8 years in DC

"Today, the global warming alarmists are the equivalent of the flat-Earthers. It used to be [that] it is accepted scientific wisdom the Earth is flat, and this heretic named Galileo was branded a denier." (03/25/15)
https://www.washingtonpost.com/news/the-fix/wp/2015/03/25/ted-cruz-compares-climate-change-activists-to-flat-earthers-where-to-begin/

"Let me be clear: Donald Trump may be a rat, but I have no desire to copulate with him." (03/25/16)
https://www.esquire.com/news-politics/news/a43332/ted-cruz-donald-trump-rat-copulate/

"Last I checked, we don't have a rubber shortage in America. Look, when I was in college, we had a machine in the bathroom, you put 50 cents in and voila." (11/30/15)
https://mashable.com/2015/11/30/ted-cruz-condoms/

"When Americans tried it, they discovered they did not like green eggs and ham and they did not like Obamacare either. They did not like Obamacare in a box, with a fox, in a house or with a mouse. It is not working." (09/25/13)
https://www.cbc.ca/news/world/why-ted-cruz-read-green-eggs-and-ham-in-the-u-s-senate-1.1867499

We saw the ugly face of radical Islam in Garland, Texas. Thankfully, one police officer helped those terrorists meet their virgins. (05/09/15) https://thehill.com/blogs/ballot-box/gop-primaries/241547-texas-shooting-showed-radical-islams-ugly-face-ted-cruz-says

"... the simple and undeniable fact is the overwhelming majority of violent criminals are Democrats." (11/30/15)
https://www.politico.com/story/2015/11/ted-cruz-planned-parenthood-democrats-crime-216288

"The scientific evidence doesn't support global warming." (12/09/15)

https://www.npr.org/2015/12/09/459026242/scientific-evidence-doesn-t-support-global-warming-sen-ted-cruz-says /

"This is not a typical moment in American history. The last 24 hours at the United States Supreme Court were among the darkest hours of our nation." (06/27/15)

https://www.upi.com/Top_News/US/2015/06/27/Ted-Cruz-Gay-marriage-ruling-makes-one-of-darkest-days-in-US-history/9301435429916/

Jesse Helms

Senator from NC from 1973 - 2003
30 years in DC

"The civil rights struggle is now no more than a political gambit leading to anarchy," Helms said in a WRAL editorial in April 1964. "It is time for politicians to stop thinking of the minority bloc votes of the next election and start thinking of the next generation. Otherwise America will be destroyed from within -- just as Karl Marx forecast." (06/10/05)
https://web.archive.org/web/20090606051301/http://www.newsobserver.com/politics/politicians/helms/story/291092.html

"I'm going to make her cry. I'm going to sing 'Dixie' until she cries.'" [Sang "Dixie" in elevator to first black female senator.] (09/06/93)
https://www.latimes.com/archives/la-xpm-1993-08-06-mn-20952-story.html

"Crime rates and irresponsibility among Negroes are a fact of life which must be faced" [said in 1981]

"Are civil rights only for Negroes? White women in Washington who have been raped and mugged on the streets in broad daylight have experienced the most revolting sort of violation of their civil rights." [said in 1963] (09/30/16)
https://www.patriotledger.com/opinion/20160930/clive-mcfarlane-politicians-given-pass-on-outrageous-utterances-about-race?template=ampart

"Look carefully into the faces of the people participating [in anti-Vietnam War protests]. What you will see, for the most part, are dirty, unshaven, often crude young men and stringy-haired awkward young women who cannot attract attention any other way." (07/05/08)
https://www.nytimes.com/2008/07/05/us/politics/05helms.html

"It is interesting to note that the Nobel Peace Prize won't be awarded this year. When one recalls that Martin Luther King got the prize last year, it may be just as well that the committee decided not to award one this year. Perhaps it was too difficult to choose between Stokely Carmichael and Ho Chi Minh." [And] "The Negro cannot count forever on the kind of restraint that's thus far left him free to clog the streets, disrupt traffic, and interfere with other men's rights." (11/27/94)
https://www.nytimes.com/1994/11/27/weekinreview/word-for-word-jesse-helms-north-carolinian-has-enemies-but-no-one-calls-him.html

Orrin Hatch

Senator from UT from 1977 - 2019
42 years in DC

"What do you call a Senator who's served in office for 18 years? You call him home." [Ran for senate with promise for term limits.] (01/03/18)

https://www.nbcnews.com/think/opinion/orrin-hatch-didn-t-need-stay-senate-republican-donors-had-ncna834246

"I probably made a mistake voting for it." (02/11/11)
http://voices.washingtonpost.com/thefix/hatch-says-bailout-vote-averte.html

"The case arose from the conduct of a small number of B.C.C.I.'s more than 14,000 employees." (08/26/92)
https://www.nytimes.com/1992/08/26/business/lawmaker-s-defense-of-bcci-went-beyond-speech-in-senate.html

"That was the stupidest, dumbass bill that I've ever seen. Now some of you may have loved [Obamacare]. If you do, you are one of the stupidest, dumbass people I've ever met." (03/01/18) https://www.sltrib.com/news/politics/2018/03/01/utah-sen-orrin-hatch-calls-obamacare-supporters-the-stupidest-dumbass-people-ive-ever-met/

"[Six years ago] it was standard practice not to pay for things." (12/25/09)
https://web.archive.org/web/20100115064248/http:/news.yahoo.com/s/ap/2009 1225/ap_on_bi_ge/us_health_care_deficit

"It will fall to the next Republican president to counteract President Obama's aggressive efforts to stack the federal courts in favor of his party's ideological agenda." (11/06/14) https://www.msnbc.com/rachel-maddow-show/gop-reconsiders-its-hatred-the-nuclear-option-right-cue-msna453836

"If we can find some way to do this without destroying their machines, we'd be interested in hearing about that. If that's the only way, then I'm all for destroying their machines. If you have a few hundred thousand of those, I think people would realize."

(06/19/03) http://usatoday30.usatoday.com/tech/news/techpolicy/2003-06-18-hatchwants-computers-dead_x.htm

"I wouldn't want to see homosexuals teaching school anymore than I'd want to see members of the American Nazi Party teaching school." (01/30/12)

https://archive.sltrib.com/article.php?id=53392378&itype=CMSID

Todd Akin

Congressman from MO 2nd District from 2001 - 2013
12 years in DC

"Don't tell anybody I'm a jail bird." [Arrested eight times between 1985 - 1989 for "peaceful" abortion protests.] (09/27/12)
https://www.youtube.com/watch?v=UV8ZAL36kfw

"And yet we have terrorists in our own culture called abortionists. Who wants to be at the very bottom of the food chain of the medical profession? And what sort of places do these bottom-of-the-food-chain doctors work in? Places that are really a pit. You find that along with the culture of death go all kinds of other law-breaking: not following good sanitary procedure, giving abortions to women who are not actually pregnant, cheating on taxes, all these kinds of things, misuse of anesthetics so that people die or almost die. All of these things are common practice, and all of that information is available for America." (10/02/12)
https://web.archive.org/web/20121007005637/http:/www.slate.com/blogs/xx_factor/2012/10/02/todd_akin_videos_cspan_clips_reveal_the_missouri_candiate_s_paranoia_about_abortion_and_stem_cell_research_.html

"Well, I think NBC has a long record of being very liberal, and at the heart of liberalism really is a hatred for God and a belief that government should replace God."
(06/28/11) https://www.foxnews.com/politics/lawmaker-apologizes-for-liberal-hatred-of-god-quip

"I've taken a look at both sides of the thing and it seems to me that evolution takes a tremendous amount of faith. To have all of the sudden all the different things that have to be lined up to create something as sophisticated as life, it takes a lot of faith." (10/12/12)
https://reason.com/2012/10/12/todd-akin-weighs-in-on-evolution/

"America has got the equivalent of the stage three cancer of socialism because the federal government is tampering in all kinds of stuff it has no business tampering in." (04/25/12) https://www.washingtonpost.com/blogs/plum-line/post/the-morning-plum-gop-backed-into-corner-on-student-loans/2012/04/25/gIQAZyohgT_blog.html

131

"Well you know, people always want to try to make that as one of those things, well how do you, how do you slice this particularly tough sort of ethical question. First of all, from what I understand from doctors, that's really rare. If it's a legitimate rape, the female body has ways to try to shut that whole thing down. But let's assume that maybe that didn't work or something. I think there should be some punishment, but the punishment ought to be on the rapist and not attacking the child." (08/19/12)
https://www.politico.com/story/2012/08/akin-legitimate-rape-victims-dont-get-pregnant-079864

"I was the target of a media assassination. ... So it really didn't matter about what I said, or logic, or truth. I had mentioned 'abortion' and 'rape.' That was enough. It was simply an assassination." (07/10/14)
https://www.politico.com/story/2014/07/todd-akin-new-book-108745

Rick Santorum

Congressman from PA 18th District from 1991 - 1995

Senator from PA from 1995 - 2007

16 years in DC

"We birthed a nation from nothing — I mean, there was nothing here. I mean, yes, we have Native Americans, but candidly, there isn't much Native American culture in American culture." (05/22/21)
https://www.nytimes.com/2021/05/22/business/media/rick-santorum-cnn.html?smid=tw-nytimes&smtyp=cur

"I've voted to kill Big Bird in the past. I have a record there that I have to disclose. That doesn't mean I don't like Big Bird. You can kill things and still like them, maybe to eat them, I don't know. That's probably that. Can we -- can we go back on that one?" [On voting to defund Sesame Street] (10/05/12)
https://www.washingtonpost.com/news/post-politics/wp/2012/10/05/rick-santorum-you-can-kill-things-and-still-like-them/?arc404=true

"We know the candidate Barack Obama, what he was like - the anti-war government nig - uh America was a source for division around the world, that what we were doing was wrong." (03/30/12)
https://www.theguardian.com/commentisfree/cifamerica/2012/mar/30/rick-santorum-slip-n-word

"I don't care what the unemployment rate is going to be. It doesn't matter to me. My campaign doesn't hinge on unemployment rates and growth rates." (03/20/12)
http://web.archive.org/web/20120322201518/http://www.chicagotribune.com/news/politics/sns-rt-us-usa-campaign-santorum-joblessbre82j0nb-20120320,0,7898443.story

"While it is no excuse for this [child sex] scandal, it is no surprise that Boston, a seat of academic, political and cultural liberalism in America, lies at the center of the storm." (07/13/05) https://www.catholic.org/featured/headline.php?ID=30

"I think I would probably tailor that a little more than what the president has suggested, that I'm not comfortable with intelligent design being taught in the science classroom. What we should be teaching are the problems and holes and I think there are legitimate problems and holes in the theory of evolution." [Contradicts 2002 statement that intelligent design should be taught in classrooms.] (08/04/05)
https://www.npr.org/templates/story/story.php?storyId=4784905

"[John McCain] doesn't understand how enhanced interrogation works." [McCain was tortured while held as POW in Vietnam.] (05/17/11) https://www.politico.com/story/2011/05/santorum-mccain-wrong-on-torture-055140

"In every society, the definition of marriage has not ever to my knowledge included homosexuality. That's not to pick on homosexuality. It's not, you know, man on child, man on dog, or whatever the case may be. It is one thing. And when you destroy that you have a dramatic impact on the quality —" [And] "The idea is that the state doesn't have rights to limit individuals' wants and passions. I disagree with that. I think we absolutely have rights because there are consequences to letting people live out whatever wants or passions they desire. And we're seeing it in our society." (04/23/03) https://usatoday30.usatoday.com/news/washington/2003-04-23-santorum-excerpt_x.htm

"I mean, you have people who don't heed those warnings and then put people at risk as a result of not heeding those warnings. There may be a need to look at tougher penalties on those who decide to ride it out and understand that there are consequences to not leaving." (09/05/05) https://www.post-gazette.com/news/nation/2005/09/06/Santorum-clarifies-Katrina-criticism-in-TV-appearances/stories/200509060141

Mitt Romney

Senator from UT since 2019
2 years in DC

"If Donald Trump's plans were ever implemented, the country would sink into a prolonged recession." [And] "Here's what I know. Donald Trump is a phony, a fraud. His promises are as worthless as a degree from Trump University. He's playing the members of the American public for suckers. He gets a free ride to the White House and all we get is a lousy hat." (03/03/16) https://www.nytimes.com/2016/03/04/us/politics/mitt-romney-speech.html

"When you have a fire in an aircraft, there's no place to go, exactly, there's no — and you can't find any oxygen from outside the aircraft to get in the aircraft, because the windows don't open. I don't know why they don't do that. It's a real problem. So it's very dangerous...." (09/24/12) https://www.latimes.com/politics/la-xpm-2012-sep-24-la-pn-romney-jet-windows-20120924-story.html

"I love this country. I actually love this state. This feels good being back in Michigan. Um, you know the trees are the right height. The, uh, the streets are just right. I like the fact that most of the cars I see are Detroit-made automobiles. I drive a Mustang and a Chevy pickup truck. Ann drives a couple of Cadillacs, actually." (02/24/12) https://www.nytimes.com/2012/02/25/opinion/blow-mitt-romney-michigan-and-a-couple-of-cadillacs.html

"There are 47 percent of the people who will vote for the president no matter what. All right, there are 47 percent who are with him, who are dependent upon government, who believe that they are victims, who believe the government has a responsibility to care for them, who believe that they are entitled to health care, to food, to housing, to you-name-it. That that's an entitlement. And the government should give it to them. And they will vote for this president no matter what...These are people who pay no income tax... [M]y job is not to worry about those people. I'll never convince them they should take personal responsibility and care for their lives." (09/17/12)
https://www.motherjones.com/politics/2012/09/secret-video-romney-private-fundraiser/

GEORGE STEPHANOPOULOS: Is $100,000 middle income?

MITT ROMNEY: No, middle income is $200,000 to $250,000 and less.

(09/14/12) https://abcnews.go.com/blogs/politics/2012/09/full-transcript-george-stephanopoulos-and-mitt-romney/

"I'm in this race because I care about Americans. I'm not concerned about the very poor — we have a safety net there. If it needs repair, I'll fix it. I'm not concerned about the very rich — they're doing just fine." (02/01/12)
https://www.politico.com/story/2012/02/mitt-i-dont-care-about-the-very-poor-072297

"Liquefied coal, gosh. Hitler during the Second World War — I guess because he was concerned about losing his oil — liquefied coal. That technology is still there." (04/20/07)
https://www.nysun.com/national/romneys-energy-gaffe/52883/

"We don't have people that become ill, who die in their apartment because they don't have insurance. We don't have a setting across this country where if you don't have insurance, we just say to you, 'Tough luck, you're going to die when you have your heart attack.' No, you go to the hospital, you get treated, you get care, and it's paid for, either by charity, the government or by the hospital." (10/11/12)

https://www.npr.org/sections/health-shots/2012/10/12/162748023/romney-people-dont-die-for-lack-of-insurance

Michele Bachmann

Congresswoman from MN 6th District from 2007 - 2015
8 years in DC

"I tell you this story because I think in our day and time, there is no analogy to that horrific action [Holocaust], but only to say, we are seeing eclipsed in front of our eyes a similar death and a similar taking away. It is this disenfranchisement that I think we have to answer to." (05/03/11) https://mndaily.com/206283/uncategorized/taxes-are-not-genocide/

"During the last 100 days we have seen an orgy. It would make any local smorgasbord embarrassed. The government spent its wad by April 26. Every dime government spends after April 26 throughout the rest of this fiscal year is borrowed money." (06/04/09) https://www.huffpost.com/entry/michele-bachmann-obama-le_n_195949

"[Pelosi] is committed to her global warming fanaticism to the point where she has said that she's just trying to save the planet. We all know that someone did that over 2,000 years ago, they saved the planet — we didn't need Nancy Pelosi to do that." (09/12/08) https://www.huffpost.com/entry/gop-rep-to-pelosi-jesus-e_n_118531

"Rather than seeing this as a negative, we need to rejoice, Maranatha Come Lord Jesus, His day is at hand. When we see up is down and right is called wrong, when this is happening, we were told this; these days would be as the days of Noah." (10/07/13) https://www.rightwingwatch.org/post/bachmann-obama-is-supporting-al-qaeda-proving-that-we-are-in-the-end-times/

"And what a bizarre time we're in, when a judge will say to little children that you can't say the pledge of allegiance but you must learn that homosexuality is normal and you should try it." (03/06/04)
https://www.coloradoindependent.com/2010/03/16/michele-bachmann-will-either-love-or-hate-the-queered-census/

"It leads to the personal enslavement of individuals. Because if you're involved in the gay and lesbian lifestyle, it's bondage. Personal bondage, personal despair, and personal enslavement. And that's why this is so dangerous." (11/06/04) https://www.tcdailyplanet.net/bachmann-will-not-seek-re-election/

"Well, what I want them to know is just like, John Wayne was from Waterloo, Iowa. That's the kind of spirit that I have, too." [Mistakes John Wayne for serial killer John Wayne Gacy.] (06/27/11) https://www.huffpost.com/entry/michele-bachmann-john-wayne_n_885368

Chuck Grassley

Congressman from IA 3rd District from 1975 - 1981

Senator from IA since 1981

45 years in DC

"I think not having the estate tax recognizes the people that are investing, as opposed to those that are just spending every darn penny they have, whether it's on booze or women or movies." (11/03/17)
https://www.politico.com/story/2017/12/03/grassley-tax-booze-women-movies-277764

"You know, I could maybe give you 10 reasons why this bill shouldn't be considered. But Republicans campaigned on this so often that you have a responsibility to carry out what you said in the campaign. That's pretty much as much of a reason as the substance of the bill." (09/20/17)
https://www.desmoinesregister.com/story/news/2017/09/20/chuck-grassley-regardless-substance-republicans-must-support-health-bill/685674001/

"If u lost ur pet pidgin /it's dead in front yard my Iowa farm JUST DISCOVERED here r identifiers Right leg Blue 2020/3089/AU2020/SHE ///LEFT LEG GREEN BAND NO PRINTED INFO. Sorry for bad news"

"I assumed deer dead bc it was night and no carcass"

"But in case of this pidgin i could actually pick up bird. No life whatsoever" (09/19/20)
https://twitter.com/ChuckGrassley/status/1307421592411156482;
https://twitter.com/ChuckGrassley/status/1307453788815536135;
https://twitter.com/ChuckGrassley/status/1307454467890122753

"I think I should be able to tell the people I'm going to be able to serve out my term. That's looking down the road six years. Maybe looking down the road six days is kind of dangerous when you're 86. But right now, I feel pretty good." (02/20/20) https://littlevillagemag.com/86-year-old-chuck-grassley-says-he-might-run-for-reelection-in-2022/

"2day is small biz Saturday I encourage all Iowans 2support Iowa small businesses if u can Small biz is the lifeblood of Main Street & this yr they've overcome many challenges incl pandemic + derecho All while supporting workers & local economies THANK U SMALL BIZ" (11/28/20)
https://twitter.com/ChuckGrassley/status/1332693769045553156

"You like to think people who are appointed to the Supreme Court respect the law." [Response to Justice Ginsburg smoking marijuana in the 60s.] (11/06/87) https://www.latimes.com/archives/la-xpm-1987-11-06-mn-12868-story.html

"You have every right to fear. You shouldn't have counseling at the end of life, you should have done that 20 years before. Should not have a government run plan to decide when to pull the plug on grandma." (08/12/09)
https://archive.vn/20120712163722/http://iowaindependent.com/18456/grassley-government-shouldnt-decide-when-to-pull-the-plug-on-grandma#selection-1921.74-1921.278

"I would welcome more women — because women as a whole are smarter than most male senators. And they work real hard, too." (10/09/18)
https://www.desmoinesregister.com/story/news/politics/2018/10/09/iowa-sen-chuck-grassley-women-smarter-judiciary-committee-women-kavanaugh-metoo-blasey-ford/1579400002/

Dan Quayle

Congressman from IN 4th District from 1977 - 1981
Senator from IN from 1981 - 1989
Vice President from 1989 - 1993
16 years in DC

"I believe we are on an *irreversible* trend toward more freedom and democracy, but that could change." (05/26/89)
https://www.wsj.com/articles/SB106263141214951400

"The Holocaust was an obscene period in our nation's history. I mean in this century's history. But we all lived in this century. I didn't live in this century. (09/15/88)
https://www.bauer.uh.edu/rsusmel/Other/Quayle.htm

"What a waste it is to lose one's mind, or not to have a mind. How true that is." (06/25/89)
https://web.archive.org/web/20040122163649/http://archives.cjr.org/year/91/5/quayle.asp

"Mars is essentially in the same orbit (as Earth's). Mars is somewhat the same distance from the sun, which is very important. We have seen pictures where there are canals, we believe, and water. If there is water, that means there is oxygen. If oxygen, that means we can breathe." (08/11/89)
https://www.washingtonpost.com/archive/politics/1989/09/01/a-quayle-vision-of-mars/f00ca97c-614b-4a9b-b14c-697adc7754f3

"Let me tell you something. As we were walking around in the store, Marilyn and I were just really impressed by all the novelties and the different types of little things that you could get for Christmas. And all the people that would help you, they were dressed up in things that said 'I believe in Santa Claus.' And the only thing that I could think is that I believe in George Bush." (11/06/88)
https://www.latimes.com/archives/la-xpm-1988-11-06-mn-423-story.html

"I was known as the chief grave robber in my state." (08/18/88) https://www.sun-sentinel.com/news/fl-xpm-1988-08-18-8802170470-story.html

"You're close, but you left a little something off. The 'e' on the end." (06/17/92) https://www.nytimes.com/1992/06/17/nyregion/the-1992-campaign-gaffes-spelling-by-quayle-that-s-with-an-e.html

"Hawaii has always been a very pivotal role in the Pacific. It is in the Pacific. It is part of the United States that is an island that is right here." [Speech given in Hawaii.] (04/21/91) https://www.orlandosentinel.com/news/os-xpm-1991-04-21-9104210345-story.html

"You all look like happy campers to me. Happy campers you are, happy campers you have been, and, as far as I am concerned, happy campers you will always be." [Speaking to group of Samoans.] (04/28/89) https://www.nytimes.com/1989/04/28/us/washington-talk-white-house.html

Clubs

Alcee Hastings

Congressman from FL 20th District since 1993

28 years in DC

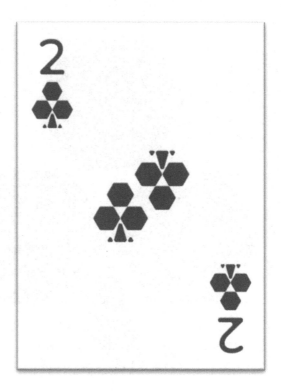

"Newt Gingrich, Sean Hannity, Ann Coulter, Michelle Malkin, Michael Barone, Drudge, anonymous bloggers and other assorted misinformed fools." (11/20/06)
https://www.seattletimes.com/nation-world/2-key-dems-passed-over-for-chair-of-house-intelligence-committee/

"Sorry, haters, God is not finished with me yet." [When Pelosi did not name him Chairman of Intelligence Committee.] (11/20/06)
https://www.seattletimes.com/nation-world/2-key-dems-passed-over-for-chair-of-house-intelligence-committee/

"If Sarah Palin isn't enough of a reason for you to get over whatever your problem is with Barack Obama, then you damn well had better pay attention. Anybody toting guns and stripping moose don't care too much about what they do with Jews and blacks. So, you just think this through." (09/25/08)
https://www.sun-sentinel.com/news/fl-xpm-2008-09-25-0809260079-story.html

"The point I made, and will continue to make, is that the policies and priorities of a McCain-Palin administration would be anathema to most African Americans and Jews. I regret that I was not clearer and apologize to Governor Palin, my host where I was speaking, and those who my comments may have offended." (09/28/08)
https://politicalticker.blogs.cnn.com/2008/09/29/black-florida-congressman-apologizes-for-comments-about-palin/

"I wish that I had been there when Thomas Edison made the remark that I think applies here: 'There aint no rules around here, we're trying to accomplish something'. And therefore, when the deal goes down, all this talk about rules, we make them up as we go along..." (03/21/10)
https://www.youtube.com/watch?v=57Vh3yUUvbg

155

"I don't know about in your state [Texas], which I think is a crazy state to begin with, and I mean just as I said it." [Continuing] "I told you what I think about Texas, I wouldn't live there for all the tea in China." (02/03/15)
https://www.youtube.com/watch?v=mlLNo48LHoM

"The way it is being framed is I participated in something secret. I wasn't in the mediation session. I wasn't part of the settlement negotiations. I secreted nothing. We need greater transparency. I personally have no objections to releasing any and all information." [Regarding $220,000 settlement of sexual harassment allegations against him.] (01/14/18)
https://www.washingtonpost.com/politics/how-a-congressional-harassment-claim-led-to-a-secret-220000-payment/2018/01/14/b3e5c6ae-dec4-11e7-bbd0-9dfb2e37492a_story.html

Ilhan Omar

Congresswoman from MN 5th District since 2019

Congresswoman from MN 5th District since 2019
2 years in DC

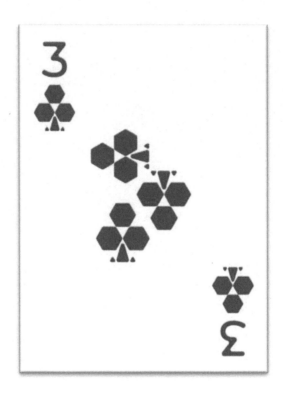

"We must have the same level of accountability and justice for all victims of crimes against humanity. We have seen unthinkable atrocities committed by the U.S., Hamas, Israel, Afghanistan, and the Taliban." (06/07/21)
https://twitter.com/Ilhan/status/1401985884191404041

"Israel has hypnotized the world, may Allah awaken the people and help them see the evil doings of Israel. #Gaza #Palestine #Israel" (11/16/12) https://www.nationalreview.com/news/rep-ilhan-omar-on-past-anti-semitic-tweet-those-were-the-only-words-i-could-think-about/

"CAIR was founded after 9/11, because they recognized that some people did something and that all of us were starting to lose access to our civil liberties." (04/11/19)
https://www.washingtonpost.com/politics/2019/04/11/some-people-did-something-rep-omars-remarks-context/

"So we cannot stop at the criminal justice system. We must begin the work of dismantling the whole system of oppression wherever we find it." (07/07/20)
https://www.washingtontimes.com/news/2020/jul/7/ilhan-omar-vows-whole-system-of-us-economy-must-be/

"Believing survivors [Biden Accusers] is consistent with my values. Yes, I endorsed against Biden and I didn't pick him as our nominee. With that said, in this interview I did on May 6th, we talked about that and quotes aren't always in context. I will vote for him and help him defeat Trump."
(05/25/20) https://twitter.com/IlhanMN/status/1264933796589326339

"It's all about the Benjamins baby." [Referring to Israeli PM Netanyahu.] (02/17/19)
https://www.washingtonpost.com/nation/2019/02/11/its-all-about-benjamins-baby-ilhan-omar-again-accused-anti-semitism-over-tweets/

159

"Let's stop normalizing + justifying state sanctioned murder by those who take an oath to uphold the law."
[Referring to Police.] (12/31/20)
https://twitter.com/IlhanMN/status/1344841158913118208

"F**k around and find out." [Selling $30 t-shirt with this slogan on her website.] (12/08/20) https://www.foxnews.com/politics/ilhan-omar-vulgar-t-shirts

Maxine Waters

Congresswoman from CA 43rd District since 1991
30 years in DC

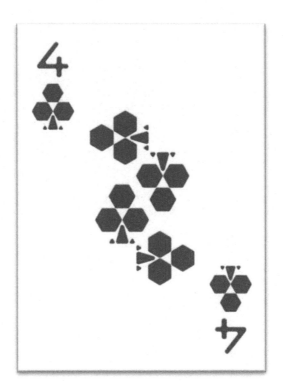

"Jussie is my friend - a very talented & beautiful human being. It is so hurtful that homophobic haters would dare hurt someone so loving and giving. I'm dedicated to finding the culprits and bringing them to justice. Jussie did not deserve to be harmed by anyone!" [Reported attack turned out to be staged.] (01/29/19)
https://twitter.com/repmaxinewaters/status/1090446736848535552

"Let's make sure we show up wherever we have to show up. And if you see anybody from that [Trump] Cabinet in a restaurant, in a department store, at a gasoline station, you get out and you create a crowd. And you push back on them. And you tell them they're not welcome anymore, anywhere." (06/25/18) https://fortune.com/2018/06/25/rep-maxine-waters-tells-supporters-to-harass-trump-cabinet-members/

"And we've got to get more active. [We've] got to get more confrontational. ... We've got to make sure that they know we mean business." (04/22/21)
https://www.msnbc.com/opinion/maxine-waters-chauvin-trial-comments-expose-democrats-hypocrisy-n1264807

"I have to march because my mother could not have an abortion." (04/26/04) https://www.nationalreview.com/corner/mad-max-kathryn-jean-lopez/

"If you call it a riot, it sounds like it was just a bunch of crazy people who went out and did bad things for no reason. I maintain it was somewhat understandable, if not acceptable. So I call it a rebellion." (05/01/92)
https://www.latimes.com/archives/la-xpm-2007-apr-29-op-wordwatch29-story.html

"This is a tough game. You can't be intimidated. You can't be frightened. And as far as I'm concerned -- the Tea Party can go straight to hell." (08/22/11)
https://www.cbsnews.com/news/rep-maxine-waters-says-tea-party-can-go-straight-to-hell/

"It is absolutely unconscionable. It is shameful, but if they would spend some time with us, we would help them to know what we're struggling for and how they would be able to help us in this struggle." [Referring to black Trump voters.] (11/1/2020)
https://www.breitbart.com/clips/2020/11/01/maxine-waters-black-trump-voters-are-shameful-i-will-never-ever-forgive-them/

Ayanna Pressley

Congresswoman from MA 7th District since 2019

2 years in DC

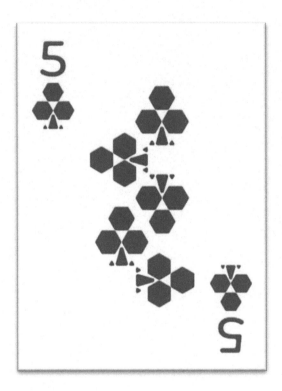

"'There needs to be unrest in the streets for as long as there is unrest in our lives,' said Pressley, D-Mass., over the weekend." (08/17/20) https://www.bostonherald.com/2020/08/17/mass-gop-takes-aim-at-ayanna-pressley-for-comments-suggesting-unrest-in-the-streets/

"I am honored & excited to be introducing my very 1st amendment on the House floor, an amendment to #HR1, the #ForthePeopleAct. My amendment will lower the voting age from 18 to 16, allowing our youth to have a seat at the table of democracy. #16toVote" (03/06/19) https://twitter.com/RepPressley/status/1103262449845776384

"Well, first and foremost, just acknowledgment of the fact that structural racism is a public health crisis." (09/11/20) https://www.wgbh.org/news/national-news/2020/09/11/rep-ayanna-pressley-calls-on-cdc-to-declare-racism-a-public-health-crisis

"This is about human and physical infrastructure. Progressives in Congress have been leading this fight. Care economy is infrastructure. Climate justice is infrastructure. Housing justice infrastructure. Public transit justice is infrastructure." (06/27/21) [5:58 AM PDT] https://archive.org/details/MSNBCW_20210627_120000_Velshi/start/3480/end/3540

"... the projections that have been offered at the American lives we could have saved if Donald Trump had not operated with willful criminality about the deadliness of this virus." (09/13/20) https://www.msnbc.com/politicsnation/watch/rep-ayanna-pressley-donald-trump-operated-with-willful-criminality-in-lax-response-to-coronavirus-91633221931

"We must be equitable in our outrage. We must abolish ICE." (06/22/19) https://pressley.house.gov/media/press-releases/progressive-congresswomen-slam-ice-and-cbp-not-one-more-dollar

"This is the time to shake that table. ... We don't need any more brown faces that don't want to be a brown voice. We don't need any more black faces that don't want to be a black voice." (07/14/19) https://thehill.com/homenews/house/453007-pressley-democrats-need-any-more-black-voices-that-dont-want-to-be-a-black

"I'm Congresswoman Ayanna Pressley, and this is a word about why my black hair story is both personal and political." [She experiences the hair loss called Alopecia.] (1/17/20) https://www.forbes.com/sites/erinspencer1/2020/01/17/rep-ayanna-pressley-beautifully-reminds-us-that-hair-is-in-fact-political/?sh=30accdf81ef3

"Student loan cancellation is a matter of racial and economic justice across our country." (12/10/20) https://finance.yahoo.com/news/student-loan-cancellation-democrat-ayanna-pressley-argues-205611285.html

"[Packing the Supreme Court] is certainly on the table." (10/24/20) https://www.bostonherald.com/2020/10/24/ayanna-pressley-says-packing-the-supreme-coourt-is-certainly-on-the-table/

Karen Bass

Congresswoman from CA 37th District since 2011
10 years in DC

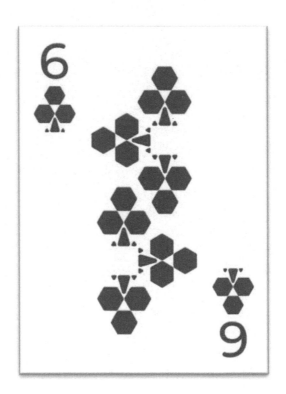

"The Republicans were essentially threatened and terrorized against voting for revenue. Now [some] are facing recalls. They operate under a terrorist threat: 'You vote for revenue and your career is over.' I don't know why we allow that kind of terrorism to exist. I guess it's about free speech, but it's extremely unfair." (06/27/09)
https://web.archive.org/web/20090630040653/http://www.latimes.com/news/opinion/commentary/la-oe-morrisonbass27-2009jun27%2C0%2C4807376.story

"I just voted to proceed on both articles of impeachment into Donald Trump. He abused the power of his office. He obstructed Congress. No one is above the law." (12/13/19) https://twitter.com/RepKarenBass/status/1205506362618331137

"Furthermore, without targeted policy changes, we can expect Covid-19 to continue to have a disproportionate impact on people of color." (11/02/20)
https://www.cnn.com/2020/11/01/opinions/trump-coronavirus-election-bass/index.html

"As Cuba begins nine days of mourning, I wish to express my condolences to the Cuban people and the family of Fidel Castro. The passing of the Comandante en Jefe is a great loss to the people of Cuba." (11/28/16)
https://bass.house.gov/media-center/press-releases/rep-bass-statement-passing-fidel-castro

"I viewed myself as speaker for the entire legislature, not just the Democrats. So I immediately had to protect him, to make sure he's okay. The press were pounding on him. I'm immediately concerned in a situation like that somebody is stable — in other words, that they don't blow their brains out or something. So that's the mode I was in, to protect him from himself and to protect him from the other Republicans, because they were ready to kill him!" (09/13/16)
https://www.washingtonpost.com/news/powerpost/wp/2016/09/13/karen-bass-says-in-politics-its-men-who-are-the-emotional-ones/

171

Eddie Bernice Johnson

Congresswoman from TX 30th District since 1993

28 years in DC

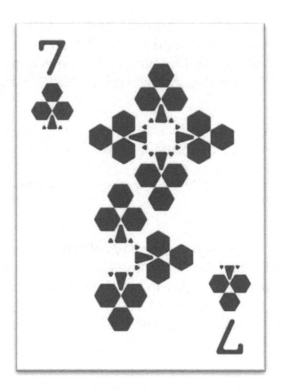

"Being a woman and being black is perhaps a double handicap, but when you see who's in the important huddles, who`s making the important decisions, it's men." (08/19/90)
https://www.chicagotribune.com/news/ct-xpm-1990-08-19-9003090294-story.html

"I am frightened to see young people who believe that a racist power structure is responsible for every negative thing that happens to them. After a point it does not matter whether these perceptions are true or false; it is the perceptions that matter." (09/10/89)
https://www.nytimes.com/1989/09/10/weekinreview/in-dallas-race-is-at-the-heart-of-city-politics.html

"I don't acknowledge, I was not around." [answered when asked 'Do you acknowledge that there was [an Armenian] genocide?] (03/11/09)
https://thehill.com/homenews/news/18702-armenian-genocide-debate-reignites

"I do deny that." [Again denies the Armenian genocide.] (05/03/17)
https://massispost.com/2017/05/architects-denial-first-person-account-armenian-genocide/

"I recognized the names when I saw them. And I knew that they had a need just like any other kid that would apply for one. [Had there been more] very worthy applicants in my district, then I probably wouldn't have given it [to my relatives]." (08/30/10) https://www.dallasnews.com/news/2010/08/30/rep-eddie-bernice-johnson-violated-rules-steered-scholarships-to-relatives/

"I know financial institutions are in it to make money. I understand that. But also, it should be something within their goals for fairness and justice for people who are not wealthy." (12/15/20) https://www.wfaa.com/article/news/local/lawmaker-financial-services-committee-to-take-up-banking-discrimination-after-wfaa-banking-below-30-story/287-8fb80669-1238-45d8-8240-88b4bce1b39b

John Edwards

Senator from North Carolina from 1999 – 2005
6 years in DC

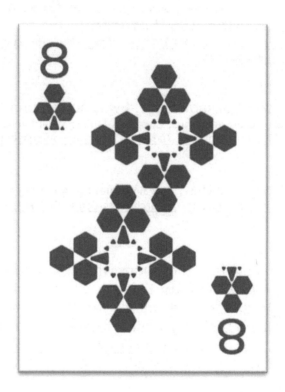

"I have no idea what you're asking about. I've responded, consistently, to these tabloid allegations by saying I don't respond to these lies and you know that ... and I stand by that." [After being caught at hotel cheating on his wife.] (07/23/08)
https://www.foxnews.com/story/guard-confirms-late-night-hotel-encounter-between-ex-sen-john-edwards-tabloid-reporters

"In 2006, I made a serious error in judgment and conducted myself in a way that was disloyal to my family and to my core beliefs. I recognized my mistake and I told my wife that I had a liaison with another woman, and I asked for her forgiveness. Although I was honest in every painful detail with my family, I did not tell the public. When a supermarket tabloid told a version of the story, I used the fact that the story contained many falsities to deny it. But being 99 percent honest is no longer enough ..." (08/08/08)
https://www.cnn.com/2008/POLITICS/08/08/edwards.statement/index.html

"I am Quinn's father. I will do everything in my power to provide her with the love and support she deserves. I have been able to spend time with her during the past year and trust that future efforts to show her the love and affection she deserves can be done privately and in peace." [Admits to fathering illegitimate child.] (01/21/10)
https://web.archive.org/web/20100123010119/http://today.msnbc.msn.com/id/34963767/ns/today-today_people/

"I never, ever thought I was breaking the law." [After being indicted for accepting illegal campaign contributions and commingling campaign funds.] (06/03/11) https://www.washingtonpost.com/politics/john-edwards-indictment-expected-today/2011/06/03/AGQwEuHH_story.html

"Can I explain what happened? First of all it happened during a period after she was in remission from cancer." [Discussing cheating on his wife.] (08/08/08)
https://abcnews.go.com/Politics/story?id=5544981

Cori Bush

Congresswoman from MO 1st District since 2021
1 year in DC

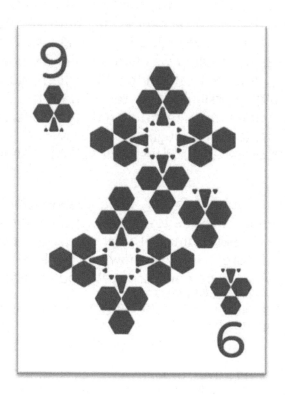

"So if I end up spending $200,000, if I spend 10, 10, 10 more dollars on it, you know what, I get to be here to do the work. So suck it up and defunding the police has to happen. We need to defund the police and put that money into social safety nets because we're trying to save lives."
(08/06/21) https://www.cbsnews.com/news/cori-bush-defund-the-police-private-security-response/

"UPDATE: There are MANY more of us demanding that the only way the bipartisan bill gets a vote in the House is if we do not miss the chance to invest in our communities with a $3.5 trillion reconciliation bill. This was already the compromise. We must deliver what we promised." (08/11/21)
https://twitter.com/CoriBush/status/1425651685133889537

"For the first time ever, the House took a vote on whether or not to end the cruelty of denying incarcerated people their right to vote. Our amendment didn't pass, but 97 Democrats voted with us. We will not stop fighting until we dismantle white supremacy in all of its forms." (03/02/21)
https://twitter.com/coribush/status/1366826151054888967?lang=en

"Our communities wouldn't have needed to spark a national movement to save Black lives if America weren't racist AF." (05/02/21)
https://twitter.com/CoriBush/status/1388960522935091206

"Take money from [police], put it into education, put money into job training programs, to address substance use issues, right?" (01/19/21) https://www.teenvogue.com/story/cori-bush-cover-january-2021

"When they say that the 4th of July is about American freedom, remember this: the freedom they're referring to is for white people. This land is stolen land and Black people still aren't free."
(07/04/21) https://twitter.com/CoriBush/status/1411713466608635909

"Today's decision to defund the St. Louis Metropolitan Police Department is historic." (04/29/21)
https://bush.house.gov/media/press-releases/congresswoman-cori-bushs-statement-mayor-tishaura-o-jones-fiscal-year-2022

Sheila Jackson Lee

Congresswoman from TX 18ᵗʰ District since 1995
26 years in DC

"Today, we have two Vietnams, side by side, North and South, exchanging and working. We may not agree with all that North Vietnam is doing, but they are living in peace. I would look for a better human rights record for North Vietnam, but they are living side by side." (07/16/10)
https://web.archive.org/web/20100718102637/http:/www.cbsnews.com/8301-503544_162-20010824-503544.html

"I'm going to be engaging you with those very powerful numbers that you have offered on what the tea party recognizes, uh, or is recognized as. Might I add my own P.S.? All those who wore sheets a long time ago have now lifted them off and started wearing [applause], uh, clothing, uh, with a name, say, 'I am part of the tea party.'" (07/16/10)
https://www.theatlantic.com/politics/archive/2010/07/sheila-jackson-lee-on-the-tea-party-and-the-klan/59888/

"You know that I'm going to first of all denounce the utilization of this intrusion by Wikipedia through the Russian intrusion." (10/21/16) https://www.washingtonexaminer.com/watch-rep-sheila-jackson-lee-confuses-wikipedia-with-wikileaks

"The temperament, the demeanor, the actions (are) in the keeping of what we try to do here in Houston... We are not rioting. We are protesting." (06/01/20)
https://www.click2houston.com/news/local/2020/06/01/we-are-not-rioting-congresswoman-sheila-jackson-lee-calls-for-even-handed-policing-amid-protests-in-houston/

"Since the initial introduction of this legislation in 1989, the importance of examining the institution of slavery in the United States has been recognized across a broad range of our society. I am pleased that Senator Booker has introduced a Senate Companion to H.R. 40. I salute his dedication to elevating the discussion of reparations and reparatory justice, and look forward to the dialogue that this issue engenders on and off Capitol Hill." (06/14/19)
https://www.booker.senate.gov/news/press/booker-reparations-bill-reaches-12-senate-cosponsors

"But unfortunately, our Congress, [specifically] the Republicans, has been dominated by the National Rifle Association, so getting guns out of neighborhoods and out of the hands of perpetrators has been very difficult ..." [No mention of Antifa or BLM violence.] (07/14/20) https://www.foxnews.com/media/sheila-jackson-lee-responds-deadly-urban-violence

Al Franken

Senator from MN from 2009 - 2018
9 years in DC

"I like Ted Cruz more than most of my other colleagues like Ted Cruz. And I hate Ted Cruz." (05/20/17)
https://ew.com/books/2017/05/20/al-franken-i-hate-ted-cruz/

"That [Antonin] Scalia's dissent [on marriage equality] was 'very gay...'" (06/02/17)
https://www.thenation.com/article/archive/al-franken-giant-senate-perfect-anti-trump/

"Listening to Mitch McConnell talk about the decline of bipartisanship is like listening to Jeffrey Dahmer complain about the decline of dinner party etiquette." (12/19/19)
https://twitter.com/alfranken/status/1207715921957138433

"[Ted Cruz is] the toxic guy in the office, the guy who microwaves fish." (05/30/17) https://www.businessinsider.com/franken-david-letterman-ted-cruz-toxic-microwaves-fish-2017-5

"At the start of the 2000 [presidential] campaign, when Bush said he was against nation-building, I didn't realize he only meant our nation." (02/23/04)
https://pitnews.com/article/35623/archives/franken-tackles-bush-hanukkah-in-husseins-palace/

FRANKEN: And I told them that I'd be a terrible office holder, so that was sort of the genesis of this idea. In fact, in the book, I become president and have to resign after 144 days.

O'BRIEN: And did you look lustfully at an intern or something? What happened?

FRANKEN: Well, I do much, much worse stuff.

O'BRIEN: Oh, Really? Like what? Oh, there's this Saddam thing; tell us about that.

185

FRANKEN: Well, what happens is during my presidency, I become depressed on day two and start getting medicated, so ...

O'BRIEN: So the honeymoon was two days.

FRANKEN: I give a disastrous inaugural address in which I apologize for slavery in a very insensitive way, and so I go through sort of bipolar behavior. During a low, for example, I punch Nelson Mandela in the stomach. (Laughter)

O'BRIEN: That's a low. That's a low.

FRANKEN: That's a low. And during a manic high, I get the idea of personally assassinating Saddam Hussein.

(01/25/99) http://www.cnn.com/books/dialogue/9901/25/franken/

Nancy Pelosi

Congresswoman from CA 12ᵗʰ District since 1987

Speaker of the House 2007 - 2011 & since 2019

34 years in DC

"What is this, a banana republic?" (06/03/20) [Report was false.] https://www.nbcnews.com/politics/congress/what-banana-republic-pelosi-unloads-trump-over-gassing-protesters-outside-n1223346

"The Chinese, they said, prefer Biden — we don't know that, but that's what they're saying, but they're not really getting involved in the presidential election. Russia is actively 24/7 interfering in our election. They did so in 2016, and they are doing so now." (08/09/2020)
https://www.politico.com/news/2020/08/09/pelosi-russia-china-election-392798

"The racist, homophobic attack on @JussieSmollett is an affront to our humanity. No one should be attacked for who they are or whom they love. I pray that Jussie has a speedy recovery & that justice is served. May we all commit to ending this hate once & for all." [He staged attack.] (01/29/19)
https://www.businessinsider.com/nancy-pelosi-deletes-tweet-supporting-empire-actor-jussie-smollett-2019-2

"I didn't know you were Catholic." [Said to congressman who kneeled to beg her not to vote for the bailout bill] (09/25/08)
https://www.nytimes.com/2008/09/26/business/26bailout.html

"Can we drill your brains?" (08/26/08)
https://www.politico.com/blogs/politico-now/2008/08/pelosi-to-protesters-can-we-drill-your-brains-011290

"You've heard about the controversies within the bill, the process about the bill, one or the other. But I don't know if you have heard that it is legislation for the future, not just about health care for America, but about a healthier America, where preventive care is not something that you have to pay a deductible for or out of pocket. Prevention, prevention, prevention—it's about diet, not diabetes. It's going to be very, very exciting. But we have to pass the bill so that you can find out what is in it, away from the fog of the controversy." (06/20/12) https://www.washingtonpost.com/blogs/post-partisan/post/pelosi-defends-her-infamous-health-care-remark/2012/06/20/gJQAqch6qV_blog.html

"I take responsibility for trusting the word of the neighborhood salon that I've been to ... many times. It was a set up. I take responsibility for falling for a set up. I think that this salon owes me an apology." [Caught without a mask.] (09/02/20) https://nypost.com/2020/09/02/nancy-pelosi-refuses-to-apologize-for-salon-jaunt-says-she-was-set-up/

"To minister to the needs of God's creation is an act of worship. To ignore those needs is to dishonor the God who made us." [Quoted fake bible verse at least 11 times on Congressional record.] (2002 - 2018) https://www.businessinsider.com/nancy-pelosi-quotes-a-bible-verse-that-doesnt-exist-isnt-in-bible-2019-2

Bernie Sanders

Congressman from VT (at-large) 1991 – 2006

Senator from VT since 2007

30 years in DC

Sanders: "You have to stop with this. I'm dealing with a fucking global crisis. You know? We're dealing with it and you're asking me these questions."

Reporter: "You're running for president, so..."

Sanders: "Well right now I'm running. Right now I'm trying to do my best to make sure that we don't have an economic meltdown and that people don't die. Is that enough to you? To keep you busy for today?"

(03/19/20) https://nationalfile.com/audio-bernie-asked-about-ending-campaign-responds-im-dealing-with-a-fcking-global-crisis/

"Now, if there is going to be class warfare in this country, it's time that the working class of this country won that war and not just the corporate elite." (08/26/19) https://berniesanders.com/podcast/ep-21-best-bernie-winning-class-war-green-new-deal-justice-all/

"The difference between my socialism and Trump's socialism is I believe the government should help working families, not billionaires." (02/09/20) https://www.axios.com/bernie-sanders-trump-socialism-7b800f30-024f-4c48-99ab-0b84d50d10d1.html

"Our bill does what the American people want by substantially increasing the estate tax on the wealthiest families in this country and dramatically reducing wealth inequality." (02/12/19) https://www.thenation.com/article/archive/bernie-sanders-progressive-estate-tax-teddy-roosevelt/

"I sometimes find it amusing when our opponents talk about the far left agenda. The truth is that when you talk about raising the minimum wage to 15 bucks an hour, when you're talking about expanding health care to all people as a human right, when you talk about effectively taking on climate change, when you talk about making public colleges and universities tuition free, these are not far-left ideas."
(11/15/20) https://www.foxnews.com/politics/bernie-sanders-far-left-agenda-supported-by-the-majority-of-american-people

"Joining every other major country on Earth and guaranteeing health care to all people as a right, not a privilege, through a Medicare-for-all, single-payer program."
(2020 [from his website]) https://berniesanders.com/issues/medicare-for-all/

"People of color in fact, are going to be the people suffering most if we do not deal with climate change."
(12/19/19) https://www.youtube.com/watch?v=5-yufjCNXEc&ab_channel=PBSNewsHour

"... because I believe we should not be selling or distributing assault weapons in this country... We've got to take on the NRA. And that is my view. And I am, will do everything I can to—" (02/18/18) https://www.nbcnews.com/meet-the-press/meet-press-february-18-2018-n849191

"If somebody commits a serious crime – sexual assault, murder – they're going to be punished. They may be in jail for 10 years, 20 years, 50 years, their whole lives. That's what happens when you commit a serious crime. But I think the right to vote is inherent to our democracy. Yes, even for terrible people, because once you start chipping away and you say, 'Well, that guy committed a terrible crime; not going to let him vote. You're running down a slippery slope."
(04/22/19) https://www.cnn.com/2019/04/22/politics/bernie-sanders-cnn-town-hall-takeaways/index.html

"When you're white, you don't know what it's like to be living in a ghetto. You don't know what it's like to be poor. You don't know what it's like to be hassled when you walk down the street or you get dragged out of a car." (03/06/16)
https://www.huffpost.com/entry/bernie-sanders-ghetto_n_56dce712e4b03a405679062b

"Some of you may agree with me, and some of you may not, but in my view, it would be hard for anyone in this room today to make the case that the United States of America, our great country, a country which all of us love, it would be hard to make the case that we are a just society, or anything resembling a just society today." (09/14/15)
https://www.washingtonpost.com/news/the-fix/wp/2015/09/14/bernie-sanders-liberty-university-speech-annotated/

Kamala Harris

Senator from CA from 2017 - 2021

Vice-President since 2021

4 years in DC

"America's position in the world has never been weaker. When democratic values are under attack around the globe, when authoritarianism is on the march, when nuclear proliferation is on the rise, when we have foreign powers infecting the White House like malware" (02/11/19)
https://www.cfr.org/blog/meet-kamala-harris-democratic-presidential-candidate

"At some point, you know, we are going to the border. We've been to the border." (06/08/21)
https://www.cnn.com/2021/06/08/politics/kamala-harris-border/index.html

"Well, listen, the idea [behind Medicare for All] is that everyone gets access to medical care, and you don't have to go through the process of going through an insurance company, having them give you approval, going through the paperwork, all of the delay that may require. Who of us has not had that situation, where you've got to wait for approval, and the doctor says, well, I don't know if your insurance company is going to cover this? Let's eliminate all of that. Let's move on." (01/29/19)
https://www.realclearpolitics.com/video/2019/01/29/kamala_harris_on_private_health_insurance_market_eliminate_all_of_that_lets_move_on.html

"Members of our military have already given so much. Raiding money from their pensions to fund the President's wasteful vanity project is outrageous. Our servicemembers deserve better." [Incorrectly claiming border wall funding would reduce military pensions.] (03/07/19)
https://twitter.com/KamalaHarris/status/1104102015897124865

"Upon being elected, I will give the United States Congress a hundred days to get their act together and have the courage to pass reasonable gun safety laws. If they fail to do it, then I will take executive action" (04/22/19)
https://www.cnn.com/2019/04/22/politics/kamala-harris-cnn-town-hall-takeaways/index.html

"'I refuse," she says vehemently, 'to design my campaign around criticizing Willie Brown for the sake of appearing to be independent when I have no doubt that I am independent of him — and that he would probably *right now* express some *fright* about the *fact* that he cannot control me. "His career is over; I will be alive and kicking for the next 40 years. I do not owe him a thing.' She acknowledges that Brown is an 'albatross hanging around my neck' and fears that voters who dislike him will ignore her candidacy — even as she dismisses such an act as irrational. 'Would it make sense if you are a Martian coming to Earth that the litmus test for public office is where a candidate is in their relationship to Willie Brown?'" [Denying that her early career intimate relationship with former San Francisco mayor Willie Brown advanced her career.] (09/24/03) https://www.sfweekly.com/news/kamalas-karma/

"It's a treat that a prisoner gets when they ask for, 'A morsel of food please,' Kamala said shoving her hands forward as if clutching a metal plate, her voice now trembling like an old British man locked in a Dickensian jail cell. 'And water! I just want wahtahhh.... Your standards really go out the f—ing window.'" (01/22/21) https://hotair.com/allahpundit/2021/01/22/wapo-erases-unflattering-anecdote-harris-18-month-old-story-n379545

Joe Biden

Senator from DE from 1973 – 2009

Vice President from 2009 – 2017

President since 2021

44 years in DC

"So the best way to get something done, if you... if you hold near and dear to you that you uh... um like to be able to... uh where am I? I'm... we're ready to get a lot done." (03/25/21) https://twitter.com/beinlibertarian/status/1375169866718658572

"'The Taliban is not the south—the North Vietnamese army. They're not—they're not remotely comparable in terms of capability. There's going to be no circumstance where you see people being lifted off the roof of a embassy in the—of the United States from Afghanistan. It is not at all comparable,' Biden insisted during a July 8 press conference." (08/15/21) https://www.newsweek.com/clip-biden-saying-people-wont-lifted-off-embassy-roof-afghanistan-resurfaces-just-that-happens-1619517

"With regard to the filibuster, I believe we should go back to a position of the filibuster that existed just when I came to the United States Senate 120 years ago." (03/25/21) https://www.washingtonexaminer.com/news/biden-jokes-120-years-experience-before-losing-thought

"I can only assume that you will enjoy educating your family about how the Coast Guard is, quote, 'The hard nucleus around the Navy forms in times of war.' You are a quiet — you're a really dull class. I mean, come on, man. Is the sun getting to you?" (05/19/21)
https://twitter.com/tomselliott/status/1395048318959562757 [and]
https://www.whitehouse.gov/briefing-room/statements-releases/2021/05/19/remarks-by-president-biden-at-united-states-coast-guard-academys-140th-commencement-exercises/

"I just want you to know that. Clap for that, you stupid bastards. Man, you are a dull bunch. Must be slow here, man. I don't know." (03/07/16)
https://www.youtube.com/watch?v=2FUcxqGObZc&t=355s [and]
https://www.reuters.com/article/uk-factcheck-biden-troops-stupid-bastard/fact-check-bidens-2016-stupid-bastards-remark-to-u-s-military-intended-as-joke-idUSKBN26L3F3

"I love those barrettes in your hair. Man, I'll tell you what, look at her she looks like she's 19 years old sitting there like a little lady with her legs crossed." [Child in elementary school.] (05/28/21) https://twitter.com/TPostMillennial/status/1398347198149152774 [and] https://nypost.com/2021/05/28/looks-like-shes-19-uproar-over-biden-remarks-about-girl-at-military-event/

"I want to thank Sec-, the former general, I keep calling him 'General.' My — the guy who runs that outfit over there." [The Pentagon chief.] (03/08/21)
https://www.washingtonexaminer.com/news/biden-flub-pentagon-chief-austin

"We have put together I think the most extensive and inclusive voter fraud organization in the history of American politics." (10/24/20) https://youtu.be/C6u1uKznCYw?t=1155

"We are in the midst of a crisis with the coronavirus. We need to lead the way with science — not Donald Trump's record of hysteria, xenophobia, and fear- mongering. He is the worst possible person to lead our country through a global health emergency." [Tweeted the day after Trump announced travel restrictions on China] (02/01/20)
https://twitter.com/JoeBiden/status/1223727977361338370

"No man has a right to raise a hand to a woman in anger." He added, "We have to change the culture. We have to keep punching at it and punching at it and punching at it." (11/21/19) https://www.nbcnews.com/politics/2020-election/live-blog/nov-20-democratic-debate-live-updates-n1087226/ncrd1088086

"What he's doing with the Uighurs in Western Mountains of China, and Taiwan, trying to end the one-China policy by making it forceful — he gets it, culturally there are different norms in each country, and their leaders are expected to follow." (02/25/21)
https://www.breitbart.com/tech/2021/02/25/watch-u-of-florida-students-shocked-when-they-hear-bidens-excuse-for-chinas-concentration-camps/

"... and Representatives Shir-Shirley Jackson Lee, Al Greene, Sylvia Garcia, Lizzie Penelley, ugh, uh, excuse me, Pannill, and, ugh, what am I doing here? I'm gonna lose track here." (02/28/21) https://pjmedia.com/news-and-politics/matt-margolis/2021/02/28/bidens-latest-verbal-slip-might-be-his-most-disturbing-yet-n1428963

"I married a Philly girl, by the way. And I've got my Eagles jacket on." [While wearing a Delaware Blue Hens jacket.] (11/01/2020) https://twitter.com/DailyCaller/status/1323021312907005962

"This is my son, Beau Biden... This is my granddaughter, Natalie. No wait, no wait. We got the wrong one..." (11/03/20) [Beau Biden died in 2015.]
https://twitter.com/Breaking911/status/1323725227487100928

"Cause if you could take care, if you were a quartermaster, you can sure in hell take care runnin' a, you know, a department store uh, thing, you know, where, in the second floor of the ladies department or whatever, you know what I mean?" (09/15/20)
https://www.realclearpolitics.com/video/2020/09/15/biden_speaks_gibberish_if_you_were_a_quartermaster_you_can_run_the_second_floor_of_the_ladies_department.html

"And, by the way, the 20, the 200 mil- the 200,000 people that have died on his watch, how many of those have survived?" (09/29/20) https://www.rev.com/blog/transcripts/donald-trump-joe-biden-1st-presidential-debate-transcript-2020

"If Donald Trump has his way, the complications from COVID-19, which are well beyond what they should be — it's estimated that 200 million people have died — probably by the time I finish this talk." (09/21/20)
https://nypost.com/2020/09/21/biden-mistakenly-says-millions-have-died-from-covid-19-in-us/

"Well I tell you what, if you have a problem figuring out whether you're for me or Trump, then you ain't black." (05/22/20) https://www.cnn.com/2020/05/22/politics/biden-charlamagne-tha-god-you-aint-black/index.html

Worker: "You are actively trying to end our Second Amendment right and take away our guns."

Biden: "You're full of sh**."

Worker: "This is not OK, alright?"

Biden: "Don't tell me that, pal, or I'm going to go outside with you, man."

Worker: "You're working for me, man!"

Biden: "I'm not working for you. Don't be such a horse's ass."

"We hold these truths to be self-evident. All men and women created by — you know, you know, the thing."

"A lot of people don't know how to register [for the COVID vaccine]. Not everybody in the community, in the Hispanic and African American community, particularly in rural areas that are distant, and/or inner city districts, know how to get online to determine how to get in line." [@16:46]

"The only way to spare more pain and more loss — the only way these millstones [sic] no longer mark our national mourning — these milestones, I should say — no longer mark our national mourning." (02/25/21)

"It's amazing. Indian-descent Americans are taking over the country — you, my vice president, my speechwriter," [And] "So be careful. You know the poor relatives, they show up. They stay longer than they're supposed to. I'm one of those kind of guys."

"We all have an obligation to do nothing less than change the culture in this country. This is English jurisprudential culture, a white man's culture. It's got to change."

"The younger generation now tells me how tough things are. Give me a break. No, no, I have no empathy for it. Give me a break. Because here's the deal guys, we decided we were gonna change the world. And we did. We did. We finished the civil rights movement in the first stage. The women's movement came to be." (01/12/18)
https://www.sfgate.com/politics/article/Joe-Biden-Millennials-2020-interview-book-tour-12494099.php

"I mean you've got the first sort of mainstream African American, who is articulate and bright, and clean and [a] nice-looking guy. I mean, that's a storybook, man." [And] "One man stands to deliver change we desperately need. A man I'm proud to call my friend. A man who will be the next president of the United States—Barack America!" (02/09/19)
www.newsweek.com/joe-biden-gaffes-quotes-2020-election-1323905/

"'You don't need an AR-15,' Mr. Biden said, referring to an assault-style rifle. 'It's harder to aim, it's harder to use, and in fact, you don't need 30 rounds to protect yourself. Buy a shotgun. Buy a shotgun.'" (02/19/13)
https://www.wsj.com/articles/BL-WB-37805

"I think the concept of busing...that we are going to integrate people so that they all have the same access and they learn to grow up with one another and all the rest is a rejection of the whole movement of black pride, is a rejection of the entire black awareness concept where black is beautiful, black culture should be studied, and the cultural awareness of the importance of their own identity, their own individuality. And I think that's a healthy, solid, proposal."
(04/25/19) www.businessinsider.com/joe-biden-anti-integration-past-resurfaces-considers-2020-presidential-bid-2019-2

"We have predators on our streets that society has in fact, in part because of neglect, created. They are beyond the pale many of those people, beyond the pale. And it's a sad commentary on society. We have no choice but to take them out of society." [1993 speech.] (03/07/19)
www.conn.com/cnn/2019/03/07/politics/biden-1993-speech-predators/index.html

"We should challenge students [with] advanced placement programs in these schools. We have this notion that somehow if you're poor you cannot do it, poor kids are just as bright and just as talented as white kids." (08/09/19)
https://www.nytimes.com/video/us/politics/100000006654886/biden-poor-kid-white-kids.html

"You cannot go to a 7-Eleven or a Dunkin' Donuts unless you have a slight Indian accent. I'm not joking." [Speaking with Indian Americans in July 2006] (10/20/15)

https://www.c-span.org/video/?c4555824/user-clip-joe-biden-7-11-gaffe

"I love Bernie, but I'm not Bernie Sanders. I don't think 500 billionaires are reason we're in trouble. The folks at the top aren't bad guys. But this gap is yawning, and it's having the effect of pulling us apart. You see the politics of it." (05/09/18) www.commondreams.org/news/2018/05/09/joe-biden-clarifies-hes-no-bernie-sanders-i-dont-think-500-billionaires-are-reason?amp

"Putin's trying to undo our elections...You think that would happen on my watch, on Barack's watch? You can't answer that, but I promise you it wouldn't have. And it didn't." [Check your 2016 calendar Joe!] (07/05/20)
https://www.breitbart.com/clips/2019/07/05/biden-russia-election-interference-wouldnt-have-happened-on-my-watch-and-baracks-watch/

"If you like your health care plan, your employer-based plan, you can keep it." [Politifacts 2013 "Lie of the Year" repeated by Biden on campaign trail.] (07/15/19) https://www.foxnews.com/politics/biden-obama-health-care-keep-it

Other "Chips"

While collecting and editing the featured quotes above, many other deserving quotes were found, but the politician did not have enough quotes to merit their own "Card." Below are some zingers from the honorable mention list.

Red Chips

Louie Gohmert, Congressman from TX, 16 years in DC:

"It reinforced the anal opening that I believe Mueller to be."

(07/01/19) https://www.politico.com/story/2019/07/01/house-republicans-robert-mueller-testimony-1385915

"'So when they want to go on a date, they invite each other to head over to the pipeline,' he informed his colleagues. It's apparently the equivalent of being wined and dined. And that has resulted in a tenfold caribou population boom, he concluded. 'So my real concern now …if oil stops running through the pipeline…do we need a study to see how adversely the caribou would be affected if that warm oil ever quit flowing?' he asked."(02/07/12)

https://www.washingtonpost.com/blogs/in-the-loop/post/louie-gohmert-best-caribou-wingman-ever/2012/02/07/gIQAIj2dwQ_blog.html

Mike Lee, Senator from UT, 10 years in DC:

"We're not a democracy." (10/07/20)
https://twitter.com/SenMikeLee/status/1314016169993670656

"Democracy isn't the objective; liberty, peace, and prospefity [sic] are. We want the human condition to flourish. Rank democracy can thwart that." (10/08/20)
https://twitter.com/SenMikeLee/status/1314089207875371008

Paul Broun, Congressman from GA, 8 years in DC:

"All that stuff I was taught about evolution, embryology, Big Bang theory, all that is lies straight from the pit of hell."

[Broun is an MD.] (09/27/12) https://www.latimes.com/nation/la_xpm-2012-oct-07-la-na-nn-paul-broun-evolution-hell-20121007-story.html

Michael Grimm, Congressman from NY, 4 years in DC:

"Absolutely not. As I said before, as long as I am able to serve, I'm going to serve." (12/23/14)
https://www.nytimes.com/2014/12/24/nyregion/rep-michael-grimm-pleads-guilty-to-tax-fraud.html

211

"I'll break you in half." (01/29/14)
https://www.nytimes.com/2014/01/29/nyregion/rep-michael-grimm-physically-threatens-a-ny1-reporter.html

"The cloud is gone. It's over; it's in the past. I've had a lot of colleagues call me and tell me they'd love to have me back." (03/28/19) https://www.politico.com/story/2019/03/28/michael-grimm-running-new-york-1241248

Ted Yoho, Congressman from FL, 8 years in DC:

"You are out of your freaking mind... Fucking bitch." (07/21/20) https://thehill.com/homenews/house/508259-ocaasio-cortez-accosted-by-gop-lawmaker-over-remarks-that-kind-of

"I can't apologize because I didn't say that." (7/21/20) https://www.news4jax.com/news/2020/07/22/rep-ted-yoho-i-cant-apologize-because-i-didnt-say-that/

"I've had some radical ideas about voting and it's probably not a good time to tell them, but you used to have to be a property owner to vote." (05/20/14) https://www.huffpost.com/entry/ted-yoho-voting_n_5360208

Trent Franks, Congressman from AZ, 14 years in DC:

"Due to my familiarity and experience with the process of surrogacy, I clearly became insensitive as to how the discussion of such an intensely personal topic might affect others." [And] "I have recently learned that the Ethics Committee is reviewing an inquiry regarding my discussion of surrogacy with two previous female subordinates, making each feel uncomfortable. I deeply regret that my discussion of this option and process in the workplace caused distress." (12/08/17) https://www.cnn.com/2017/12/07/politics/trent-franks-statement-analysis/index.html

212

Tim Murphy, Congressman from PA, 14 years in DC:

"I did not see its toxicity until I was months into [the relationship]."

(11/27/16) https://www.post-gazette.com/news/politics-nation/2017/10/03/rep-tim-Murphy-pro-life-sought-abortion-affair-shannon-edwards-susan-mosychuk-pennsylvania-chief-of-staff-congress-emails-texts/stories/201710030018

"I get what you say about my March for life messages. I've never written them. Staff does them. I read them and winced. I told staff don't write any more. I will." (01/25/17) https://people.com/politics/republican-congressman-retirement-after-abortion-scandal/

"The United States is one of just seven countries worldwide that permits elective abortion more than halfway through pregnancy (beyond 20 weeks). It is a tragic shame that America is leading the world in discarding and disregarding the most vulnerable." (01/24/17) https://www.post-gazette.com/news/politics-nation/2017/10/03/rep-tim-Murphy-pro-life-sought-abortion-affair-shannon-edwards-susan-mosychuk-pennsylvania-chief-of-staff-congress-emails-texts/stories/201710030018

Blue Chips

Pete Stark, Congressman from CA, 40 years in DC:

Stark: "Get the fuck out or I'll throw you out the window!" [And] "The more debt we owe, the wealthier we are."

Stark: "Give me that tape or I'm going to punch your lights out!"

Hanfeld: "Take it easy I only ask you a few questions."

Stark: "Give me that God damn tape." [Threatened interviewer after cameras cut.] (08/23/08) https://www.youtube.com/watch?v=UjbPZAMked0

Bobby Rush, Congressman from IL, 28 years in DC:

"[Barack Obama] went to Harvard and became an educated fool. Barack is a person who read about the civil-rights protests and thinks he knows all about it."(11/09/08)
https://www.newyorker.com/magazine/2008/11/17/the-joshua-generation

Marcia Fudge, Congresswoman from OH, 13 years in DC:

"Lance accepts full responsibility for his actions and has assured me something like this will never happen again." [And] "The Lance T. Mason I know is a kind intelligent man and loyal friend." [After Mason brutally attacked his wife in front of their kids. (He later murdered his wife.)] (08/09/15)
https://www.cleveland19.com/2018/11/20/congresswoman-marcia-fudge-releases-statement-lance-mason-whom-she-defended/

Hank Johnson, Congressman from GA, 14 years in DC:

"My fear is that the whole island [of Guam] will become so overly populated that it will tip over and capsize" (04/01/10)
https://www.cbsnews.com/news/hank-johnson-worries-guam-could-capsize-after-marine-buildup/

"'There has been a steady [stream], almost like termites can get into a residence and eat before you know that you've been eaten up and you fall in on yourself,' he said, according to The Washington Free Beacon. 'There has been settlement activity that has marched forward with impunity and at an ever increasing rate to the point where it has become alarming'" (07/24/16) https://thehill.com/blogs/blog-briefing-room/news/289125-dem-rep-israeli-settlers-are-like-termites

Cashing in their Chips

In addition to the pay and substantial benefits described in the first chapter, the Members of both houses are able to parlay their inside knowledge into personal fortunes. This is all the while most claim to be over-worked and under-paid. Not all Members are successful at this part of the game, and some have spouses who reportedly provided the gains. This spouse part is questionable since reporting requirements, while vague, do require disclosures of personal financial information. This encourages some of the Members to "separate" their finances from their spouses, so part of their family's finances can go unreported.

Reported below are some of the Members and their families. Some have rather significant wealth and others justify a fuller disclosure of their finances.

Disclaimer: Since there is no fully accurate report on the wealth of each Member and how they acquired it, there are no definitive sources that reveal the absolutely true picture. Predictably, the reporting is often by partisan news sources which have an axe to grind with one party or the other.

Further, discussion here of the wealth, real or apparent, of the Members mentioned, does not mean that they did anything illegal. Of course, in some cases, illegal or unethical conduct may have been involved. It is up to the US court system to make those determinations. This book addresses the "court of public opinion."

Nancy Pelosi
Net Worth Range - $34 million to $242 million

The "Queen of Clubs" likes to portray the Democratic Party as the party of the downtrodden in our society. Looking down from her wealthy perch, that is not a very credible position.

"The California Democrat is worth an estimated $114 million, according to her 2018 personal financial disclosure, making her one of the wealthiest members of Congress." [And] "Federal lawmakers report a range for their wealth but not exact amounts. That means the maximum amount that Pelosi had in assets in 2018 was $257 million and the maximum had she had in liabilities was $97 million, making her net worth no higher than $160 million. At a minimum, Pelosi has $54 million in assets and $20 million in liabilities, for a net worth of about $34 million."[37][38] Note that California is a Community Property state, meaning that whether assets are shown on her disclosure or attributed to her husband, she still owns half of everything gained during her marriage.

An interesting article from 2011 shows how what is legal can still be highly questionable if fully disclosed:

> *House Minority Leader Nancy Pelosi's husband, a real estate developer and investment banker, stands to make millions of dollars in a*

---

[37] https://www.foxbusiness.com/money/how-much-money-is-nancy-pelosi-worth
[38] See: https://disclosures-clerk.house.gov/public_disc/financial-pdfs/2018/10026982.pdf

previously undisclosed residential real estate project in California as a partner with the father of a woman Mrs. Pelosi helped become ambassador to Hungary, records show. [And, the article concludes:] In a 2010 interview, Mr. Pelosi said there was "no connection" between his business dealings and his wife's role in helping Mrs. Tsakopoulos-Kounalakis become ambassador. "There is no story here," he said. "My business dealings have nothing to do with my wife's political career."[39]

Despite the fact that at her advanced age, she is unlikely to be able to spend all that she already has, Pelosi is still doing deals to make even more money. One that raised eyebrows was buying "call options" on Tesla stock later in 2020. The obvious significance of this is the Biden administration's push for electric vehicles and even a commitment by the Feds to convert the entire US fleet of 645,000 vehicles to electric.[40] As the head of the US Congress, she is directly involved in such government policies that would obviously help those options increase in value. Pelosi did disclose her option purchase.[41]

There is some controversy about whether the Members can legally use their inside knowledge of what will be financed or what permits will be granted by various federal and state authorities. In 2012, the Stock Act was passed: "To prohibit Members of Congress and employees of Congress from using nonpublic information derived from their official positions for personal benefit, and for other purposes."[42] To date, it does not seem to have had much impact, although some Members have actually been investigated. There is no report of a Member

---

[39] (10/10/11)
https://www.washingtontimes.com/news/2011/oct/10/pelosis-disclosure-belated-in-husbands-land-deal/
[40] (01/27/21) https://www.yahoo.com/entertainment/nancy-pelosi-recent-stock-purchase-173817407.html
[41] See: https://disclosures-clerk.house.gov/public_disc/ptr-pdfs/2021/20018011.pdf
[42] https://www.congress.gov/112/plaws/publ105/PLAW-112publ105.htm

being prosecuted for insider trading as of the date of this publication. The definition of "non-public" may be part of the issue. While certain important information may be available to the public, being both the first to know about certain corporate or economic developments and then being in a position to anticipate the impact affords the Members a substantial head start.

Dianne Feinstein
Net Worth Range - $55 million to $120 million
(Possibly $1 billion+)

The "Queen of Spades," another fantastically wealthy Democrat, is hard to evaluate accurately since she separates her assets from her husband, Richard Blum. He is the owner of a private equity firm named for him and could be worth $1 billion or more.[43] Again, a Californian, where marital assets are Community Property.[44] CBS Sacramento published indication of her wealth.[45] Feinstein did disclose stock deals involving Nvidia, FedEx and 3M.[46][47]

Newt Gingrich
Net Worth Range - $6.7 million to $31 million

The "4 of Hearts," a Republican, was the top politician in the country 1994 to 1999, other than Bill Clinton. His 2010 report shows a convertible promissory note worth up to $25 million from the Gingrich Group, LLC to Gingrich Productions, Inc. Report also shows a debt to Tiffany & Co. for up to $1 million while showing his ownership in Gingrich Productions

---

[43] https://en.wikipedia.org/wiki/Richard_C._Blum
[44] https://efdsearch.senate.gov/search/view/paper/6b337c7f-4fd6-45f8-a18f-04c0fcded472/
[45] https://sacramento.cbslocal.com/2021/06/28/sen-dianne-feinstein-tahoe-vacation-compound-for-sale-41-million/
[46] https://www.barrons.com/articles/dianne-feinstein-nvidia-fedex-stock-husband-richard-blum-51550598246
[47] For the disclosure itself, see: https://sec.report/Senate-Stock-Disclosures/FEINSTEIN/DIANNE/aaafdc5d-4641-4a0a-9f6c-31333bab4d6e

valued up to $1 million, plus $2.4 million in distribution shares and a $300,000 salary.[48][49] In contrast, his 1997 report showed a net worth of less than $1 million.[50] Gingrich's wife, Callista, former US Ambassador to the Holy See, brings in a yearly salary of $242,005 from Gingrich Productions, and also owns a considerable interest in this company, listed at $250,000 up to $500,000.[51] In commenting on his 2010 report, the *Los Angeles Times* noted: "That's a considerable jump from 2006, when financial disclosures filed by Callista Gingrich reported the couple's net worth at between $873,000 and $2.4 million."

Kamala Harris
Net Worth Range - $1 million to $16 million
The "Ace of Clubs," a Democrat, has an amazing wealth story given her mostly public positions throughout her modest career. Her 2020 financial report shows two mortgage balances of up to $5 million each, several millions of assets in mutual funds and retirement accounts, and several hundreds of thousands earned in the past couple years from book deals.[52] Note that this financial report combined the income with her husband, entertainment lawyer Douglas Emhoff. Forbes published an interesting discussion of the couple's net worth.[53]

[48] http://pfds.opensecrets.org/N00008333_2010_pres.pdf
[49] http://pfds.opensecrets.org/N00008333_2010_tax.pdf
[50] http://pfds.opensecrets.org/H6GA06033_97.pdf
[51] https://www.documentcloud.org/documents/4388236-Callista-L-Gingrich-Financial-Disclosure.html
[52] https://www.whitehouse.gov/wp-content/uploads/2021/05/Harris-Kamala-D.-2021-Annual-278.pdf
[53] https://www.forbes.com/sites/michelatindera/2021/06/11/heres-how-much-kamala-harris-is-worth/?sh=387b89911303

Harry Reid

Net Worth Range - $3 million to $10 million

The "Five of Spades," a Democrat, is reported to have improved his financial position while in Washington. Having retired in 2012, some of the background on him is a bit dated. Coincidentally, his net worth seemed to peak around 2012 when he was serving as NV Senator.[54]

> *In 2004, the senator made $700,000 off a land deal that was, to say the least, unorthodox. It started in 1998 when he bought a parcel of land with attorney Jay Brown, a close friend whose name has surfaced multiple times in organized-crime investigations and whom one retired FBI agent described as 'always a person of interest.' Three years after the purchase, Reid transferred his portion of the property to Patrick Lane LLC, a holding company Brown controlled. But Reid kept putting the property on his financial disclosures, and when the company sold it in 2004, he profited from the deal — a deal on land that he didn't technically own and that had nearly tripled in value in six years.[55]*

And, referring to Member stock trading practices as noted above, Reid profited from the 2005 purchase of Dow Jones U.S. Energy Sector Fund (IYE) for $29.15/share.[56] In 2008, he sold the shares for $41.82, but a month later, proposed a bill that would be costly for the oil companies. The

---

[54] https://www.opensecrets.org/personal-finances/harry-reid/net-worth?cid=N00009922&year=2015
[55] https://www.nationalreview.com/2012/08/how-did-harry-reid-get-rich-betsy-woodruff/
[56]

http://finance.yahoo.com/echarts?s=IYE+Interactive#symbol=iye;range=20051209,20080829;compare=;indicator=volume;charttype=area;crosshair=on;ohlcvalues=0;logscale=off;source=undefined;

stock dropped to $24.41, so Reid was either a wonderful investor, or had access to just the right information.[57] Note that another publication ran a correction regarding this transaction: "Reid's office responded: 'Senator Reid's stocks are held in a blind trust over which he has no control,' adding, that 'ethics experts have long recommend broad-based funds over individual stock ownership.'"[58] The National Review article also referenced a real estate deal that netted Reid some healthy appreciation, and that he was in a position to influence its value by obtaining ear-marked funds:

Theoretically, working as a lawmaker should have severely limited Reid's earning potential. In the early 1980s, members of Congress received a salary of about $70,000 per year. Though pay has generally risen -- and Reid receives more than most lawmakers because of his leadership position -- he has never earned more than $200,000 per year in salary. [And] Yet, his estimated net worth peaked at around $10 million just a few years ago, and he has remained consistently wealthier than when he entered Congress.[59]

John Kerry
Net Worth Range - $66 million to $250 million
(Possibly $1.2 billion)

The "Two of Spades," a Democrat, Kerry's fortune is tied to his marriage to Teresa Heinz, widow of a Heinz Company heir, with an estimated net worth between $700 million - $1.2

[57] https://www.nationalreview.com/2012/08/how-did-harry-reid-get-rich-betsy-woodruff/
[58]
https://www.realclearpolitics.com/articles/2014/04/24/harry_reids_long_steady_accretion_of_power__wealth.html
[59]
https://www.realclearpolitics.com/articles/2014/04/24/harry_reids_long_steady_accretion_of_power__wealth.html

billion.[60] It is reported that Teresa Heinz has a pre-nuptial agreement with Kerry. A good part of Kerry's personal wealth was acquired by inheritances of trusts through his mother's family.[61]

Kerry's net worth was estimated at $103 million in 2013, but this was a big decline from the 2012 estimate of $236.51.[62] It is notable despite his visibility in public campaigning for renewable energy, that he is reported to have had significant investments in energy stocks.[63]

Chuck Grassley
Net Worth Range – $2 million to $24 million

The "King of Hearts," a Republican, filed a detailed financial report indicating a net worth that could vary from $2 million to $24 million, but given other information, probably leans to the higher number.[64]

Grassley operated a family farm with his son Robin for years. He indicated that he would accept President Trump's federal farm bailout cash, calling it "equal treatment."[65] And Grassley applied for farm bailout cash for the second time when

[60] https://en.wikipedia.org/wiki/Teresa_Heinz

[61] https://www.foxbusiness.com/markets/john-kerrys-net-worth-what-to-know

[62] https://www.opensecrets.org/personal-finances/net-worth?cid=N00000245

[63] For Kerry's most recent available financial records, see: https://www.documentcloud.org/documents/20694598-john-kerry-financial-disclosure

[64] (05/17/21) https://efdsearch.senate.gov/search/view/annual/6dc791b1-c2ad-4c7a-82db-fe961d842977/

[65] https://www.desmoinesregister.com/story/news/politics/2018/10/03/iowa-chuck-grassley-donald-trump-trade-farm-china-bailout-cash-federal-soybeans/1512757002/

the program was again offered.[66] The Environmental Working Group, or EWG, is a non-profit that specializes in environmental research. This group maintains a database of USDA subsidies. EWG records show Grassley's son, Robin, accepting $1.3 million in USDA subsidies from 1995-2019.[67] Grassley's latest 2020 financial disclosure shows farmland sold to Robin in 2020.[68]

For instance, Senate financial records show Grassley made consistent income from his farms from 2013 through 2020 ranging from $100,000 up to $2 million per year despite accepting government bailouts in 2018 and 2019.[69]

> *"Many taxpayers would be shocked to learn members of Congress who are receiving what by any measure is a lot of money are now also receiving a bailout check ostensibly designed to help struggling farmers," Faber said. "It underscores exactly what's wrong with the bailout program — that many of the recipients of farm bailout funding are doing just fine."[70]*

Mitt Romney
Net Worth Range - $76 million to $276 million

The "Jack of Hearts," a Republican, has a well-publicized history as a big money player before entering politics. He went into the consulting business after earning a JD and MBA from Harvard. He eventually became CEO of Bain

---

66
https://www.desmoinesregister.com/story/news/politics/2019/05/24/chuck-grassley-seek-federal-farm-bailout-cash-offset-donald-trump-tariffs-china-trade-war/1209374001/
67 https://farm.ewg.org/persondetail.php?custnumber=A07143444
68 https://efdsearch.senate.gov/search/view/annual/6dc791b1-c2ad-4c7a-82db-fe961d842977/
69 https://bipartisanreport.com/2018/10/01/millionaire-chuck-grassley-takes-tax-money-from-farm-bailout/
70 https://www.washingtonpost.com/business/2018/09/28/sen-charles-grassley-apply-bailout-money-farmers-under-white-house-program/

Capital and helped that company through some tough times to become a very successful operation which made him a millionaire many times over. He phased out his operation of Bain Capital in 2001 to help Salt Lake City host the 2002 Winter Olympics. His net worth at that time was estimated to be $200 million to $250 million. From there, he moved into politics, first as the Governor of Massachusetts from 2003 to 2007.[71]

He has remained active in politics since that time, becoming a US Senator from Utah in 2019. His most Recent Financial Report (2019) indicates that he has sizable investments and still takes in millions in current income from those investments.[72] He has filed an extension request as of this writing for filing his 2020 report. There is no indication that his extensive personal estate specifically profited from his short time in the US Senate.

Rick Santorum
Net Worth Range - $700,000 - $5 million

The "10 of Hearts," a Republican, he left the Senate in 2007 after losing in the 2006 election. A report on his finances was published for 2010[73] Since he was a presidential candidate in the 2012 primary, his latest report is for 2014.[74] The reports show a shift from rental real estate to a fascinating listing of stocks in various companies, many of them "tech" stocks.

---

[71] https://en.wikipedia.org/wiki/Business_career_of_Mitt_Romney
[72] https://efdsearch.senate.gov/search/view/annual/6ba23276-e8cd-4b3c-b425-94233986b216/
[73] http://pfds.opensecrets.org/N00001380_2010_pres.pdf
[74] http://pfds.opensecrets.org/N00001380_2014_Pres.pdf

Michele Bachmann
Net Worth Range - $1 million to $3 million

The "Queen of Hearts," a Republican, she was also a presidential candidate in the 2012 primary. She was a member of Congress from 2007-2015. She did not run for reelection in 2014.[75] Her husband's Christian counseling practice and a family farm from his side of the family is included in her combined disclosure statement.

Joe Biden
Net Worth [Estimated] $8 million

The "Joker," a Democrat, appears to have profited from his years as a Member before becoming VP, and of course, later President. There is no official document that ties his net worth together, but a June 2021 Forbes article put his estimated net worth at $8 million.[76] The most interesting part of the article was a discussion of his lifelong spending habits and that he should be worth much more. Given the spending surge he brought to the White House, then, this should be no surprise.

He reportedly brought in $17 million from speeches and books sales in his time out of office from 2017 to 2020, but financial reports for those years are unavailable on his official website.[77] His presidential campaign site does link to this report.[78] However, it also has a link that goes to a donation site for Act Blue, a Democrat fund-raising operation.[79]

Not only do the candidates and their spouses appear to get special financial benefits for being a Member, but certainly

---

[75] https://disclosures-clerk.house.gov/public_disc/financial-pdfs/2015/9106040.pdf

[76] https://www.forbes.com/sites/michelatindera/2021/06/10/heres-how-much-joe-biden-is-worth/?sh=16f07807461b

[77] https://www.forbes.com/sites/michelatindera/2020/10/22/how-the-bidens-earned-167-million-after-leaving-the-white-house/?sh=22c7c7221e42

[78] https://joebiden.com/wp-content/uploads/2020/05/OGE-Form-278e-signed.pdf

[79] https://secure.actblue.com/donate/legacy-donate-bfp

children and others close to the Members also benefit. No report on capitalizing on a Member's position would be complete without a discussion of Joe Biden's son, Hunter Biden, and others. Quoting from a key Senate report:

> On April 16, 2014, Vice President Biden met with his son's business partner, Devon Archer, at the White House. Five days later, Vice President Biden visited Ukraine, and he soon after was described in the press as the "public face of the administration's handling of Ukraine." The day after his visit, on April 22, Archer joined the board of Burisma. Six days later, on April 28, British officials seized $23 million from the London bank accounts of Burisma's owner, Mykola Zlochevsky. Fourteen days later, on May 12, Hunter Biden joined the board of Burisma, and over the course of the next several years, Hunter Biden and Devon Archer were paid millions of dollars from a corrupt Ukrainian oligarch for their participation on the board.[80]

The advantage of being the son of a VP and former senator did not end there for Hunter Biden:

> During the Obama administration, the Committee on Foreign Investment in the United States (CFIUS) approved a transaction that gave control over Henniges, an American maker of anti-vibration technologies with military applications, to a Chinese government-owned aviation company and a China-based investment firm with established ties to the Chinese government. One of the companies involved in the Henniges transaction was a billion-dollar private investment fund called Bohai Harvest RST (BHR). BHR was formed in

---

[80]https://www.hsgac.senate.gov/imo/media/doc/Ukraine%20Report_FIN AL.pdf (page 3)

November 2013 by a merger between the Chinese-government-linked firm Bohai Capital and a company named Rosemont Seneca Partners. Rosemont Seneca was formed in 2009 by Hunter Biden, the son of then-Vice President Joe Biden, by Chris Heinz, the stepson of former Secretary of State John Kerry, and others.[81]

Other relatives can also get into the act. See:

Ye's connections to the Communist government are extensive and, as explained below, he has been previous affiliations with the People's Liberation Army. Based on the information received by the Committees, Ye was also financially connected to Vice President Biden's brother, James Biden. Thus, there exists a vast web of corporate connections and financial transactions between and among the Biden family and Chinese nationals.(p. 71) [And] On the same day that the impending Rosneft deal was announced, Hunter Biden and Gongwen Dong, a Chinese national who has reportedly executed transactions for limited liability companies controlled by Ye Jianming, applied to a bank and opened a line of credit under the business name Hudson West III LLC (Hudson West III). Hunter Biden, James Biden, and James Biden's wife, Sara Biden, were all authorized users of credit cards associated with the account. The Bidens subsequently used the credit cards they opened to purchase $101,291.46 worth of extravagant items, including airline tickets and multiple items at Apple Inc. stores, pharmacies, hotels and

---

[81]

https://www.hsgac.senate.gov/imo/media/doc/Ukraine%20Report_FINAL.pdf (page 3). [Footnote omitted]

228

restaurants. The cards were collateralized by transferring $99,000 from a Hudson West III account to a separate account, where the funds were held until the cards were closed. The transaction was identified for potential financial criminal activity.[82]

It is unmistakable that the Biden family profited from his political positions. Further, while he continues to deny any involvement, the evidence seems quite strong that he was fully aware of many of the key pieces of such deals, even if he did not personally manage them.

[82]

https://www.hsgac.senate.gov/imo/media/doc/Ukraine%20Report_FINAL.pdf (pages 76-77) [Footnotes omitted]

Conclusion

Our Founding Fathers believed in a real democracy where the government did the bidding of the people. America is far from that today. In order to have civilian legislators that come from the people, stay connected to the people and serve the people's interest, we must have substantial reforms. Millionaires who hang out mostly in the rare air of Washington, DC, are paid well above the average American's income, and abuse their positions for years are not representative of the "average American." The game is power and gaining more power seems to be the key focus of many of the so-called representatives of the people. The initial step is to try to elect far more responsive members for both houses of Congress. In obtaining term limits, it is hoped that enlightened, new members of Congress will voluntarily do so and limit their pay and benefits. Since I am not Pollyanna, I anticipate a Convention of the States may be required to achieve effective term limits.[83]

---

[83] https://conventionofstates.com/

Public Records Access on Member Financial Reports

For readers that would like to look up the official public financial reports filed by the Members, see:

Members of Congress:

- https://disclosures-clerk.house.gov/PublicDisclosure/FinancialDisclosure

Members of the Senate:

- https://sec.report/Senate-Stock-Disclosures
- https://www.ethics.senate.gov/public/index.cfm/financialdisclosure
- https://efdsearch.senate.gov/search/home/

Acknowledgements

Bad Deal for America is the culmination of two years of research and effort. While I wrote the book and did much of the research myself, I had significant help with researching, citations, and editing. My two lead researchers for much of this project were Richard "Ricky" Dittemore, presently a JD candidate at the South Texas College of Law, and Rebecca "Becca" DeFreese McAlister, a recent graduate of the University of Houston. Several others, including Alaina Ursin and Taylor Philip Colaiacomo, current or former students at the University of St. Thomas-Houston, helped with research on various chapters and their time and efforts are also appreciated. I especially want to thank Rachel Harrison for providing numerous editorial suggestions as well as being the long-time Office Manager for Claremont Management Group. She is also the Producer of my *Saving America* webcasts, which helps to promote my writing projects. I want to thank my family and friends who have encouraged me along the way. It is also my pleasure to introduce Mike Lin, the fine artist who helped to highlight and bring this book a unique "pop."

As always, the content and intent of this book is my responsibility, not my wonderful researchers, editors or the publisher.

About the Author

David D. Schein is a Professor and the Cameron Endowed Chair of Management and Marketing for the Cameron School of Business at the University of St. Thomas-Houston. He is also an author, speaker, attorney, and consultant. He speaks on human resource and business matters for industry groups throughout the United States. He is also known as a political and business commentator through his regular webcasts, *Saving America* and *Business Law 101*. He is frequently quoted in national and regional publications with his views on numerous hot button issues. Dr. Schein focuses on practical, common-sense solutions. His book, *The Decline of America: 100 Years of Leadership Failures*, was released by Post Hill Press on Presidents' Day 2018 and has garnered numerous favorable reviews. He holds a BA from University of Pennsylvania, an MBA from University of Virginia, a JD from University of Houston, and a Ph.D. University of Virginia.